THE GOVERNMENT NEVER SLEEPS

What the government's been up to while you were sleeping and why you need to wake up NOW!

J. Paul Henderson

CATO GROUP

ISBN-13: 978-0615537603
ISBN-10: 061553760X
LCCN: 2011938507

Dedications:

In memory of my father, Bob, the *original* "Robbie D", who taught me valuable lessons, each one of which I learned the hard way.
I know why.

In memory of my mother, June, Justine or whatever she's calling herself in the big cookbook in the sky.
Everyone who knew her knows why.

The late Karl Hess, with thanks and admiration
He taught me everything I needed to know about writing in one day.

Special thanks to:

Syd, for the ongoing encouragement and help
Morris, for never giving up on me
Roger, for being patient
Sal, for enduring the things I find interesting

CONTENTS

PART THREE: LIVING IN AMERIKA

Introduction

The United States and our freedom and prosperity are all but gone. By now, this should be obvious, unless you've been living on another planet or you're still refusing to take the red pill.

The purpose of this book isn't to try to convince you things are bad and getting worse. Let's just agree that they are and they are. At this point, nothing short of a long-shot election day miracle has the slightest chance of saving what's left of our once great republic.

Winning freedom is extremely difficult. Keeping it requires some effort. But losing it is easy. The problem is that we chose the easy road. Because we weren't willing to put forth the effort to *keep* our freedom, we'll now have to do difficult and possibly risky things to win it back.

This book is divided into three parts. In part one I'll discuss a few aspects of American history. History you didn't learn in school, even if you *were* paying attention. Because the government runs the schools and only teaches you what it *wants* you to know: what's in *its* best interest.

And in our little history lesson, you'll learn things -- important things -- not in the best interest of those who want to control you and steal your wealth. Important things. Things left out of your history textbooks because they *are* important. To *you*.

Why the history lesson? Because as a wise man once said, "Those who don't learn the lessons of history are doomed to repeat them." You can't understand where you are until you understand where you were.

The second part of the book explains the true nature of government. All governments. And the kinds of people who aspire to political office, and what their true motives are. Hint: It's not because they care about your children, your safety or your health. Government is an exclusive club, and you're not in it.

It's in the second part of this book that the plot thickens. This is where you'll learn how politicians, bureaucrats, corporations, and banks have all cooperated to increase their power and wealth at your expense. You can't defeat your enemy until you've identified him. The enemy isn't stupid people in Washington. It's *smart* people in Washington who are counting on *your* being stupid.

In this part of the book you'll learn what they've been up to while you were busy watching "American Idol", and what they have planned next. Knowing what was, what is, and what's coming will help you know what to do to hold on to or win back your liberty and prosperity.

And that brings us to part three. Unless we turn the ship around, and *fast*, the last of our freedom and what's left of our prosperity *will* be gone. The boot of the leviathan is about to be felt on our necks, and in ways more unpleasant than you can imagine.

If this country ends up where it's on a collision course for now, life is going to get very different, very quickly. In part three you'll learn how to adapt to what's coming, how to be secure in your home and how to hold on to at least a little bit of your privacy. I'll give you a variety of strategies to survive and protect yourself from the forces that have worked, schemed and conspired to reduce your existence to serfdom.

When you're finished reading this book, give a copy to your children, your neighbors, your coworkers or anyone else you care about, whose eyes need to be opened, so they won't be doomed to what the past three generations have allowed to happen. Give them a fighting chance for a good life.

Empires always fall. The Roman Empire, the Ottoman Empire, the British Empire, the Soviet Empire and all the others, fell. They fell because people like you and me --

8

freedom loving people -- chipped away at their edges and created cracks that grew to become fissures that destroyed the foundations of the empires, causing them to implode on themselves.

But this time is different. Because for the first time in known human history, the bad guys have technology. Technology to spy on those of us whose only desire is to live free and be in charge of our own lives. Caesar and Stalin only wished they had the power to listen to everyone's phone conversations, read everyone's emails, track everyone's movements with GPS, track everyone's purchases with credit cards and RFID chips and watch their every movement with thirty million hidden cameras.

Fortunately, we have access to some of the same technology. Good thing; we'll need it.

Lastly, a little bit about your intrepid purveyor of Truth.

I'm not an economist. I'm not a sociologist. I'm not a historian. At least not formally. I hold no degrees of higher or lower learning. I left high school early. Not because I couldn't keep up with the curriculum; rather, because the curriculum was impeding my education.

I've read more than two thousand books and have had the great fortune of having some very smart and learned people as mentors. And in my years as an investigative journalist I learned how to look under the rocks and find the slime, that the emperor ain't got no clothes and that the man behind the curtain is not the great and powerful Oz.

There are no footnotes in this book. No references. I began my quest for Truth when I was in the ninth grade. It's been a passion, bordering on an obsession ever since. *I've done my homework. I've researched and analyzed meticulously.* If you have a problem accepting any of the information in this book, do your own homework. Prove me wrong. It'll be easier for you than it was for me. You have the Internet.

And lastly, while nothing in this book is untrue, the book is full of attitude. And the more my freedom is taken away the worse my attitude becomes. You don't need to think as I do, but you need to start thinking for *yourself*. Next time you hear the "official" line, take some time and ask yourself, "*Does this make sense?*"

One thing you can do to learn the art of critical thinking is to turn off the TV news. In fact, just turn of the TV, period. There's little worth watching, anyway.

As you begin thinking for yourself, you'll probably find that many of your ideas will differ from those of your friends or coworkers. That's because *you'll* be the one doing the thinking. I'll never forget something my father said to me when I was a child: "If a million people believe a stupid thing, it's still a stupid thing." And these days, millions of people believe stupid things.

Love freedom? Want it back? Want your children to have a better life?

Okay. Let's get started.

Part One: The Birth of Liberty

The Seeds of Discontent

If you read ten books about the American Revolution, you'll get ten different versions of the story. Was it strictly economic? All about taxes? Oppression from the British Crown? Religious freedom? It was all those things and more. The American Revolution was the right thing, at the right time, in the right place. Mostly, *it was possible*.

One thing we do know is that the revolution wasn't a popular uprising. Only about twenty-five percent of the colonists were in favor of revolution. The rest were either loyal to the Crown or had no strong opinion, one way or the other. But twenty-five percent is more than enough for a good, rip snortin' revolution.

One thing that did unite the colonists was the desire for basic human rights. The right to keep the fruits of their labor, the right to worship or not worship God in any way they chose, the right to live their lives as they chose as long as they weren't infringing on the rights of others, and the right to be left alone.

One thing on which almost all historians can agree is that those at the forefront of the revolution were some of the most brilliant people in all of history. The Federalist Papers, the Anti-Federalist Papers, Cato's Letters, Poor Richard's Almanac and other writings of the time were filled with thought-provoking ideas. These people were learned and insightful. They were philosophers. They weren't writing about mundane political issues; they were sharing ideas.

And the one idea in common was that being free is better than not being free. A very revolutionary idea at the time.

What it came down to is that either the King would acknowledge and honor basic human rights or be prepared for a fight. The King called the colonists' bluff.

The reason England lost the Revolutionary War is the same reason the Roman Empire fell and the same reason the United States can't win the war in Afghanistan. It's hard to win a war against people who just want to be left alone. Especially if you're fighting them on their own turf.

The Romans called their adversaries terrorists. We call the Afghans terrorists. And the British Crown called the American revolutionaries terrorists. But one person's terrorist is another person's freedom fighter.

The revolutionaries just wanted to be left alone and live their lives freely and peacefully. They wanted to trade with each other voluntarily, to raise their children as they saw fit, and to acquire a little bit of property without having it taxed or regulated out from under them.

Not a lot to ask in the grand scheme of things.

So the King sent in his armies and navies, the biggest and most powerful in the world at the time. They had the *big* guns. But the colonists were on their own turf and really, *really* wanted to be left alone.

So in marched the Red Coats, with all their armaments. And our rag-tag, poorly trained and equipped army of guerrilla warriors eventually managed to pick them off with hunting rifles, booby traps, rocks or anything else at their disposal. They lost their share of battles, but they didn't give up.

The short version of the story is they won.

And it's at this point when the real history of America begins.

We won! We weren't a nation; we were a bunch of loosely governed former colonies. We could have pretty much stayed that way, as the Anti-Federalists probably would have preferred. Or we could form some sort of union. A federation of states.

The idea of a federation of states carried the day and a constitutional convention was called to figure out how to put it all together. There wasn't unanimity of opinion. There was plenty of wrangling, arguing and jockeying for position. But one thing they could all agree on was a concept learned from the American Indians: government by the consent of the governed.

Many of the Indian nations had a governmental structure alien to Europeans: The chiefs had no police power. They only governed as long as they had the *respect* of those they governed. If the chief lost the respect of his people, he had to step down.

Talk about a great concept. If Congress had to govern that way today, they'd all be back home now, doing *honest* work for a change. But I digress.

The point is that this concept made a lot of sense to the Founding Fathers. They wanted to craft a constitution that made it very difficult for a government to get out of control and assert police powers over the people.

Here's what they did: Things glossed over for about twenty minutes in American History class.

Did they give us a national government? No. Did they give us a democracy? No. Did the Constitution grant us any rights? No. No? No.

The founders, or their parents, coming from Europe,

knew all too well what always happens when the government acquires too much power, and they were determined to make sure it didn't happen here.

What the founders gave us was a federation of states, not one nation-state. We weren't a country; we were thirteen countries bound by a treaty called the Constitution. That's why we were called the United *States* of America. A state is an autonomous entity. Germany is a state. Israel is a state. Brazil is a state. What the Constitution gave us was not unlike what the European Union is today. In fact until not that many years ago, people referred to the union as *these* United States (plural), not *the* United States.

We were the United States. Not the United Political Subdivisions.

How much power did the federal government have over the citizens? None. Zip. Zilch. Nada. The Constitution only lists three federal crimes: Counterfeiting, treason and piracy. That's it. If you weren't printing your own money, conspiring against the federation in time of war or hijacking something, the feds had *no* power over you.

All other governing and policing was the responsibility of your state or the town in which you lived. The founders knew that the only way to keep government from getting out of hand was to keep it small and close to home where people could keep a watchful eye on it.

And what form of federal government did they give us? A democracy? Hardly. The Founding Fathers were fearful of democracy. They considered it to be tyranny of the majority. Potentially as dangerous as a dictatorship. They understood that most people know little or nothing about economics, the law or diplomacy. That being the case, why should they be voting? Our founders realized that if they gave us a democracy, eventually guests of the Jerry Springer Show would have a voice in government equal to that of normal people.

"What?" you say. Democracy is good. It means freedom. It's majority rule. What could be more fair than that?

The truth is that there's nothing inherently fair about democracy and the founders knew it. What makes the majority fair or right? In a democracy, if fifty-one percent of the people want to do something absolutely ridiculous, the other forty-nine percent still have to obey. Is that fair? Is that freedom? Democracy is nothing more than two foxes and a chicken voting on what to have for breakfast. In a republic, *who's* in charge of things isn't nearly as important as *obeying the rules* is.

So the founders gave us a republic. A set of rules the state had to abide by. A constitution. What the Constitution amounted to was a social contract. The citizens drew up a contract, formed a government, and told it, in effect, "This is what we're going to allow you to do. This and only this."

And to help keep the federal government in it's place, they put it *outside* the United States. They carved out a few miles of not very desirable land along the Potomac and created the District of Columbia. Washington, DC is technically not *in* the United States. Have you ever wondered why residents of Washington, DC aren't allowed to vote? They don't live in the United States. They didn't teach you *that* in American History, did they?

According to the Constitution, the only power the federal government had (unless you were printing money in your basement) was over the states. And even that power was quite limited. The primary functions of the federal government were maintaining free and fair commerce among the states, coining money, defending the states in time of war and maintaining a supreme Court. And on that subject, the purpose for the court was to determine if someone had violated the Constitution, not to interpret it. The Constitution didn't need a bunch of judges to interpret it; it was written so clearly that any sixth grader could understand it.

One of the things the Constitution says, that any sixth

grader can understand, is if it ain't in there, the government can't do it. It gives the federal government a short list of things it's allowed to do -- and nothing else. It's right there. It says so.

For a number of years, I taught school. One of my classes was on the Constitution. I always began that class by asking my students who could vote for president, according to the Constitution. I was amazed at the answers I got. White people. Males. People over twenty-five. Property owners. The correct answer is nobody. At least not the way we think of voting today. There's nothing in the Constitution about the people voting for President. Go ahead. Look it up.

The President was elected by the Electoral College. The electors represented the *states*. The electors may have been appointed or nominated by the state legislatures and could be voted for within the states. Each state had its own policy on elections and representation. But if you were a male over twenty-one and chose to vote, and not that many people did, you voted for people to represent your state. The electors chosen from each state voted for the president. The president was elected by 535 people. The President and the people had a lot of distance from each other.

And this made sense, because the President was the President of *the United States*, not the President of the *people*. He had no real power over the people. And back then, most people didn't much care who the President was because very little he did had any direct effect on them.

Guess what? You couldn't vote for your Senator, either. The Senate was an *appointed* office. The purpose of the Senate was to protect the rights and interests of the states. *Your* state.

You could vote for your Congressman in the House of Representatives. The House of Representatives was the *peoples'* House. The House is where each Congressman represented a small area and the peoples' voice could be heard. Again, keeping government close to home where people could keep an eye on it. This is why all "money bills" -- legislation requiring the government to spend any money -- has to originate in the House. According to the Constitution, the Federal Government can't spend any money unless the people *allow* it to.

And what about our rights? Didn't the Constitution grant us rights, like, say, freedom of speech? No. Governments can't grant rights. Your rights come from God, or if you prefer, because you exist. You have a *natural* right to speak your mind, to worship or not worship the god of your belief, to defend yourself, and any number of other things that don't interfere with the rights of others. The Bill of Rights, attached to the Constitution, said the people *already had* those rights and the Constitution was to prevent the government from taking your rights away.

And what *is* a right? Basically a right is being at liberty to do anything you want to do as long as you're not stealing or defrauding someone, or thumping someone on the head in order to accomplish what you want. This means you have the right to think what you want, write what you want, complain about the government if you want, eat and drink what you want, smoke what you want, wear what you want, marry who you want, and a lot of other things. If someone else is forced to act on your behalf, it's not a right. Exercising your natural rights can't infringe on the rights of anyone else.

For decades, the government has been working overtime to take your rights away. A little bit at a time. It just chips away at them. A little here, a little there. The one they *really* want to take away is the right secured in the Second Amendment: the right to keep and bear arms. The government would have us believe the founders wanted to make sure we could go hunting or target shooting. The truth is they wanted us to be able to protect ourselves from the government, if and when it decided to take the rest of our rights away. The true purpose of the Second Amendment was to ensure the citizens could protect themselves from their own government if it became oppressive. Which it has.

If the colonists practiced gun control, we couldn't have won the revolution, could we? The government knows this, which is why it would love to have you turn in your gun. For your own good, of course.

The whole concept of natural rights has been so perverted today that it's no wonder so many people don't understand what rights are. Today we have gay rights, black rights, women's rights, air travelers' bills of rights, welfare rights, ad nonesensium. These aren't rights; they're merely *privileges* designed to garner favor from various voting blocks and win elections. One of the dangers of democracy.

Because the federal government was very limited in its powers, we had great diversity. Immigrants came here from many different places, and each group brought its own religious and social customs. And because people from different countries tended to settle with their own kind when they arrived here, the culture here varied from one part of the country to another. The customs, beliefs, morals and attitudes in New England weren't quite the same as those in the southeast or mid Atlantic area.

So each state would enact its own legislation, reflecting the lifestyles and beliefs of its citizens. If you didn't like the state you lived in, you could move to another one. And it would be *different*. And because each state wanted to attract settlers and a healthy business base, they were competitive with each other. Any state that taxed too heavily or otherwise made life unpleasant would lose population.

And because the government left us alone to live as we pleased, because taxes were *very* low, and because states competed for population and business, we prospered. In very short order, we became the wealthiest people in the history of the world. The poorest of Americans lived better than most of the rest of the world.

What the American experiment in liberty proved was that when people are free to live as they please, they'll live, for the most part, in peace, and they'll prosper. They'll work, they'll build, they'll invent. They'll create a great life and a great society -- naturally.

But that was then, and this is now.

What happens when Bubba from the trailer park wins a million dollars in the lottery? About twenty minutes later, people line up at his door with nifty things to sell him or dazzling investment schemes. Six months later, they have his money and he'll be broke again. The same kinds of people who would conspire to get Bubba's lottery winnings, would also like to have your freedom and your property.

What we'll learn later on is what happens when people are set free. There are a lot of people in the world who aren't very nice. People who would steal from you if they could. People who would control you if they could. People who would love nothing more than to take your freedom and place themselves in positions of power. There are always enemies of freedom.

They may be the head of your labor union, the leader of your church, the CEO of the company you work for, or the person who wants your vote on election day. You may think these people would never cooperate with each other, but you'd be wrong. It's all about power, money and control of your life.

The enemies of freedom never divulge their true agenda. They all promise to do good things for you -- as long as you give them your money and grant them more power. Hitler was the popularly elected president of Germany (so much for the goodness of democracy). He didn't get elected by promising to kick some ass, kill some Jews, confiscate businesses and go to war. He promised the German people he'd do lots of good things for them if they'd just give him some more power. We all know how that turned out.

So the Founding Fathers gave us something wonderful. Something unique in all the world. A federal government that maintained order, defended us from invasion, coined honest money for trade, maintained a court to punish those who would violate our constitution, protected our natural rights and...

And that's about all. We were free to live our lives as we pleased, and to prosper if we could. Such a deal!

But no sooner was the ink dry on the Constitution than people who weren't very nice became busy conspiring to take our freedom away, enriching and empowering themselves in the process.

And that brings us to the next chapter, in which I'll discuss some of the early attempts to take your freedom away from you. If you want to win back your freedom, you first have to know how you lost it. If you don't, even if you win it back, you'll just end up losing it again.

Planting the Seeds of Tyranny

There have been so many times and so many ways that efforts have been made to transfer freedom and wealth from the people, to those who'd rather steal than earn, that to cover them all in detail would require several volumes. So I'll highlight just as few of them with the hope that you'll see how these early efforts opened the doors to the wholesale destruction of our liberty underway today.

The Central Bank

The first was the idea of a central bank. This concept was promoted from the first days of the republic, by Alexander Hamilton and others. I have no way of knowing if Hamilton actually believed a central bank was a good idea, or if he was consciously acting on behalf of the powerful bankers behind the scene.

The promotion of central banks began with Mayer Rothschild, a wealthy banker in Germany. Rothschild and his five sons established themselves in important capitals and money centers throughout Europe and worked for the creation of central banks in several countries. Banks the Rothschilds would control and profit from. Having control of the economies of entire countries gave their banking dynasty immense political power, as well. Mayer Rothschild was once quoted as saying, "Give me power over a nation's money supply and I care not who writes its laws."

The Rothschilds and other powerful banking interests were salivating over the prospect of being in control of what was sure to become the world's biggest economy.

But the constitution made no mention of a central bank. Instead, it gave Congress the power to coin money and determine its value. And that's what it did. The government minted coins, mostly from gold and silver. A one-ounce silver coin represented one dollar, and a one-ounce gold coin was valued at twenty dollars.

Since it wasn't very convenient to carry a lot of heavy coins around in one's pocket, banks printed paper money. This wasn't like the paper money of today; it was a *receipt* for actual gold or silver on deposit. You could trade it in for the real thing any time you wanted.

In short, our financial system was relatively honest and fairly stable.

But it wasn't making anybody rich. There's a lot of profit and power when you control the creation and issuance of all the money in a country and the powerful European bankers were eager to sink their teeth into America's emerging wealth.

Early on, a central bank was established: The First Bank of the United States. It didn't take long for the people and the honest politicians (there were a few in those days) to realize this was a bad deal, and the bank was dissolved after a few years. But that didn't stop the bankers. They just came back with something "new and improved": The Second Bank of the United States. But in truth, the second bank wasn't an improvement; it was simply the first bank with a new grille and taillights.

Andrew Jackson was elected President in 1828, and he was the central bankers' worst enemy, calling the bank the worst "engine of corruption" in the country. Failing to dissolve the bank, he ended up just refusing to renew its charter.

And from that time until 1913, the United States did just fine without a central bank. But in 1913, the central banking interests had their ducks all in a row and managed to get the necessary legislation passed in Congress in the dead of night, when many members had left to go home for the winter holidays. Quickly and quietly while nearly no one was looking.

That was the Federal Reserve Act. The Federal Reserve may be the *biggest* enemy of your freedom and prosperity. In the second part of this book, I'll explain how the Central bank operates and how it created massive debt that you'll spend your entire life paying back...

Unless.

The point is that the enemies of liberty have been around since the founding of the republic, and the banking elite have been out to get your money since day one.

Slavery and the Civil War

Like much of the rest of American history taught in schools, the story of slavery and the war that was supposedly fought to end it was composed largely of lies.

There's little argument that the institution of slavery was the biggest stain on the history of our country. One of the worst crimes against another person is taking his labor by force, in essence, *owning* him.

But slavery wasn't unique to our country; slavery had been practiced all over the world throughout human history. The ancient Egyptians engaged in slavery, as did the Romans, Europeans, Africans, some of the American Indians. And others.

And in spite of a hundred years of propaganda to the contrary, slavery was *not* a racial thing. The slave owners didn't enslave people because they were black. For the most part, they bought *existing* slaves. At the time, northern Africa was the world's leading exporter of people already captured and enslaved. It was a lot easier and more economical to buy an existing slave than to go to the effort to capture someone and enslave him.

Not all black people were slaves and not all slaves were black. True, the great majority of the slaves came from Africa, but it was a matter of economics, not racism. Some of the slaves were white and some were American Indians. In fact, before the Civil War, there were many free *black* slave-owners in the south.

Further, and this is something conveniently left out of high school history books, there were slaves in the north, too. In the north they worked in textile mills and factories, rather than on farms. One of the bloodiest slave uprisings was in *New York City*.

Then there's the falsehood taught in schools that the Constitution only considered black people as three-fifths of a person. The fact is that there's no mention of race in the Constitution. The Constitution says that for *the purposes of apportionment*, slaves were to be counted as three-fifths of a person. Enslaved whites and Indians were counted as three-fifths of a person, and free blacks were counted as a whole person.

One of the concepts to emerge from the Age of Enlightenment was the idea that owning someone's life and livelihood was a despicable practice. And over time, slavery was abolished in most of the world. Peacefully.

Except here. We fought the bloodiest war in our history over slavery. At least that's what we were told. The truth is slavery was not the cause of the Civil War; it was merely the *excuse*.

People are reluctant to go to war without a good reason. To fight the evil Nazis, to fight the vicious commies, to fight the Muslims over there so we don't have to fight them here, to spread democracy around the world -- or to abolish slavery. There's always an emotional reason, which is never the *real* reason. And the American Civil War, or the *War of Northern Aggression* as southerners more accurately describe it, was no exception.

Prior to the Civil War, we were still independent states that had voluntarily joined a federation called the United

States. Here's the sticky issue: If a state volunteered itself *into* the federation, did it have the right to volunteer itself *out*?

Many people then and to this day believe the southern states had no right to secede. Once you join the club, you're in for life.

Let's examine the morality of this. Think of the state as just a big version of yourself. And as such it shouldn't be allowed to do anything *you're* not allowed to do. If you believe the north was right in invading the south after secession, ask yourself this: Let's say you joined the Chamber of Commerce. After a while you became disillusioned with its policies and decided not to renew your membership. Should other members of the Chamber be allowed to go to your house and start shooting at you?

Why not? What's the difference?

The truth is that the southern states seceded over taxes and tariffs, not slavery. Left to their own devices, the southern states would likely have abolished slavery on their own -- peacefully -- as had been happening all over the world at the time. The problem was that through a variety of taxes and import policies and restrictions, the southern states were getting their lunch eaten by the industrial states of the north. Had the south been allowed to peacefully secede, over time the states probably would have resolved their differences with the south eventually rejoining the union.

But Lincoln wanted a war. What? Honest Abe, who grew up in a log cabin, did his studying by candlelight and as a child walked a hundred and fifty miles uphill in the snow to return a library book? *That* Abraham Lincoln? The Lincoln for whom we have a giant granite memorial in Washington with an enormous likeness of him looking down at us?

Yeah. *That* Lincoln. For the most part, the presidents most memorialized are the ones that did the most harm to the greatest number of people. The state loves power.

Lincoln wanted a war and so did the bankers. Banks *finance* wars, which can be very profitable.

Did Lincoln care about the slaves, or for that matter, black people? Let's ask Lincoln. What did Lincoln think of black people? The now dreaded awful "N" word was a regular part of his vocabulary. He just couldn't stop saying "nigger". He said he'd still have fought the war even if it meant *not freeing a single slave*. And in fact, after the war, he gave serious consideration to deporting the then freed slaves and sending them to what is now Belize in Central America. How's all that for being a good friend of black folks? If I were a black person living back then, I would not have wanted Abraham Lincoln as my next-door neighbor. Not without a good fence and a pit bull.

But Lincoln was more than a racist and a warmonger. He was also a ruthless, bloodthirsty tyrant. He put hundreds of newspapers out of business. Disagree with his policies and you were toast. And he operated prison camps, much like Gitmo or the secret CIA prisons around the world today.

Disagree with Lincoln's policies and he'd send his henchmen out to round you up and put you in one of his prison camps. Charges? He didn't need no stinkin' charges, since he also suspended habeas corpus. And if you really got under his skin, he'd just have you executed. No need for a trial or conviction. Trials took time and the country was at war.

And during Lincoln's reign of terror, thousands of innocent Americans died of disease, malnutrition or starvation in the prison camps.

By the time he was assassinated, Lincoln was more feared and hated than George W. Bush and Barack Obama *combined*. By all means, let's build a big memorial to this guy. Interestingly, the Republicans like to refer to themselves as "The Party of Lincoln". That ought to tell you something about the Republicans.

What Lincoln left in his wake was a deeply divided

people, nearly three quarters of a million dead Americans, the complete devastation of the south and massive war debt.

He sent hoards of Yankees into the south to involve themselves in "reconstruction". Corruption, election rigging and violence were rampant. Already destroyed by the war, the southern economy wasn't helped by the interference of the carpetbaggers from the north and it took many years to recover. It also caused great bitterness toward the north, which among some southerners lingers to this day.

And Lincoln left another legacy. He showed that a president could engage in corruption and gross violations of the Constitution, to say nothing of basic human rights-- *and get away with it.*

He established a precedent. If Lincoln could do evil things and not be held accountable, so could the next president...or the next.

States Rights

So Lincoln opened the door to federal intrusions into our lives. But we still had one safeguard: The United States Senate. Remember, the Senate was an appointive office, the purpose of which was to represent the interests of the *states*. This created some degree of resistance to the growing federal beast. We were still the United *States* of America.

There was a way around this pesky little problem, too. A constitutional amendment. This one changing the Senate from and appointive office to an elective office. More democracy.

With the ratification of the seventeenth amendment in 1919, the last vestige of federalism bit the dust. Instead of Senators being appointed by the state legislatures to represent the interests and sovereignty of the states, senators were now elected, just like members of the House. Senators now weren't much different from members of the House of Representatives; they just had a bigger territory. So much for half of Congress representing the states, with the other half representing the people -- one of the very thoughtful checks and balances the framers of the Constitution built into it for our protection.

It was all about democracy from that time on. You remember what democracy is, don't you? Two foxes and a chicken voting on what to have for breakfast? With the Senate now an elective office, *different* kinds of people aspired to a seat there. Rather than people who were interested in the law, economic issues and the rights of the citizens of their states, candidates for office were politicians. People with a thirst for power, personal wealth and notoriety. People who'd promise everything and say anything you wanted to hear to win your vote.

While there were a plethora of things, great and small, that the government and the banks did to chip away at Americans' liberty and wealth, I chose to discuss these three because I feel they were particularly egregious and destructive. These were some of the poisonous seeds of tyranny, planted early in our history.

In Part Two of this book, you're going to learn what's been happening in more recent times, and in great detail. You'll learn about the *true* nature of government, who really owns the Federal Reserve (Hint: It's not Federal), how and why we got the personal income tax, why the dollar bill you hold in your hand now only buys four cents worth of goods or services, why all government programs fail, who *really* writes the bills your elected representatives vote on, why we seem to have so many enemies, how we went from a free republic to a democracy to an empire, how banks and big business have all conspired with the government to separate you from your freedom and your money, what they plan to do to you next, and a lot more.

By the time you're finished with Part Two, you should be angry enough to be ready for Part Three.

Part Two: The Death of Liberty

What is Government?

The Contract

This might be the first time you've even read the Constitution. It's important that you read and understand it, because it's the contract between you and the federal government. It spells out in very clear language what the government *can't do to you*. Because if it's not in the contract, the government can't do it. That's the law. And every time the government does something that violates the contract, it's committed a criminal act against you.

If there's something in the contract the people want to change, it can be amended. But when the provisions of the contract are just ignored, you end up with what we have now: an out-of-control government run amuck.

Right now you might be thinking, what about education? Roads? Help for poor people? Do you not believe your own state could build its roads? Or that your own community couldn't raise enough money to build its schools? Or that religious institutions and charities wouldn't care for the less fortunate? It's the way it was always done until the past fifty or sixty years.

The Founding Fathers realized that things are done best when they're done close to home. That's why the constitution clearly states that authority or activity not specifically granted to the federal government is to be left to "the States or the people"

That means us.

Next I'm going to shatter some myths about what government is and isn't. Then we'll take a look at some of the unconstitutional things the government has been up to and how these activities have brought us to where we are today: a corrupt empire on the verge of bankruptcy.

What is Government, Really?

To understand the true nature of government, and the difference between good government and bad government, you need a good foundation in morality. A lot of morality occupies a gray area, but there are a few things on which we can nearly all agree. For example, Murder is wrong, as is stealing or lying for personal gain. Once government goes beyond its legitimate functions, everything it does includes theft, fraud or killing.

And these are all things that can land us in prison if we do them. Being convicted of murder, theft or fraud can get you a lot of years in a depressing place populated by very unpleasant people.

But once government crosses the line from the things it has a moral right to do, everything it does would put you and me in prison if *we* did it. What does *that* make the government? In the next chapter, I'm going to itemize things the government does that would put us in prison if we did them. Criminal acts.

But before I get into the many things the government does, but shouldn't, I want to share four important myths about government with you right now.

Myth #1: The government is us.

Is the government *us*? No, the government (as it currently operates) is *them*.

First, it's important to understand the difference between a nation and a state. They're not the same thing. A nation is a group of people of similar heritage, customs and language, who occupy a reasonably well-defined area. The American Indians were nations, but not states. You may also look at nations as tribes.

You may have wondered why the names of so many countries in Central Asia end in "stan". Pakistan, Afghanistan, Uzbekistan, etc. Originally, these were nations, or tribes. "Stan" means settlement. The Afghan settlement, the Uzbek settlement, etc. Like the American Indians, and many other people around the world, what held these societies together were the cultural things they had in common.

We still have Indian nations within the United States. They're not states, they're nations: people with a common heritage and culture living together. In a somewhat more loose sense of the word, we might consider Jews to be a nation -- not matter where in the world they live. They're bound by culture. Or Mormons. It wouldn't be too much of a stretch to think of the inhabitants of Utah as a nation. These are peoples with a distinct culture unique onto themselves.

A state is something different. The Soviet Union was a state. It gobbled up a couple dozen nations and forced them to live by its laws and pay taxes to it. Nations in which the people had little in common with each other, including language.

The concept of the nation-state is relatively new in human history. A nation, such as the Jews or the Mormons, or for that matter, the American Indians, the Amish or the people of the "stans" didn't need a government. At least not much of one. They just kind of held together and cooperated.

With the rise of the state, people of different cultures were forced to live together under the thumb of a central government. When the United States was comprised of many small states, bound together in a federation, each state retained its culture and governed according to the wishes of its own people. This is why the laws in New York, for example, were somewhat different from those in, say, South Carolina. Different cultures.

But now we've become one big nation-state with everyone bound by the same laws. One size fits all. Yet are we really one nation? Depending on our cultural background, we don't listen to the same music, eat the same food, practice the same religion, or even speak the same brand of English. But the now central government dictates that what's good for one is good for all.

But in a nation-state, what the government is really concerned about is what's good for *it*. We may be a nation, but we're not the state.

How many times have you heard someone refer to the government as "of the people, by the people and for the people"? It's as if they think this is something official. Like maybe from the Declaration of Independence or something. It's simply a line from Lincoln's Gettysburg Address, and we already know how much Lincoln cared about the people.

Government is really all about government. Your primary function is to give it money. Money it squanders on itself and it's rich corporate friends.

Let's take a look at the current economy. To get everything moving again, we got a trillion dollar "stimulus package". Where did all the money go? It went to big banks -- even foreign banks. It went to rich corporations. It created vast new government bureaucracies. Do you feel stimulated? Doing better now? What happened to all those "shovel-ready" projects? Where are all the new jobs, other than in Washington? The money's all been spent. How much of it did *you* see? The "stimulus" was nothing more than the government committing a trillion dollar fraud and theft. It lied, it stole.

You see, it's never about *you*; it's always about *them*.

Daily, we're told we have to tighten our belts. Drive less in cheap small cars. Re-adjust our thermostats. Learn to get by on less money.

Meantime, in the cesspool on the Potomac, everything's fine. Lavish parties, fancy vacations, dinners in four star restaurants. The bureaucracy is getting bigger, fatter and richer. And the average federal employee makes (I don't want to say "earns") nearly twice what he would make in the private sector. Big salaries and fat pensions. At your expense. In fact, Washington, DC is a boomtown. It's growth central USA.

This may come as a surprise to you, but it costs Americans more money to keep the President than the Brits spend on the Royal Family. Lyndon Johnson used to brag that every time he left the White House, it cost a million bucks. And he was right.

When Barack Obama has to go somewhere, he doesn't climb into a corporate-type jet and take off. He flies (everywhere) in a custom-made 747. And along with him is a fleet of helicopters, another plane full of staff and servants, and cargo planes full of his special fleet of limousines. And when he gets wherever he's going, they close the roads to the folks who pay the bills so the president can have the highway all to himself. Well, himself and his huge entourage.

And while we're tightening our belts and eating Spam, our rulers are hosting fancy parties with the best Champaign and exotic foods. And I meant "rulers". Because that's what they are. Do you really believe while they're living their grand life, that they're giving a moment's thought to your children?

Your job is to pay *their* bills.

Myth #2: Your representatives are in Washington to serve you.

Your Congressman and Senator (and for that matter, the President) have two employers -- and you're not one of them. Their first employer is the government. And the government's mission is to take in and spend more money and increase its power. Every freshman Senator or Representative learns this on day one. Their second employer is the special interests that ponyed up millions of dollars to get them elected. That money isn't a donation; *it's a bribe*.

35

It's been estimated that the 2012 presidential election will cost a *billion dollars.* Whose interests to you think the next president will be serving? Yours or the people who wrote those fat checks?

Your only function is to believe the lies -- or campaign rhetoric, as they're euphemistically referred to -- and give them your vote.

Myth #3: There's a difference between Republicans and Democrats.

Here's something interesting. And it's true. The human mind can't reject two things at once. It can reject one, three or a dozen, but not two. We're just hard wired that way.

So we have a "two party system". And it's sold to us as if it was handed down by God, or something. And within that two party system, we have liberals and conservatives. We even have blue states and red states. You live in one or the other. And have you noticed that public policy is always sold to us as either this or that? We never get this, that or another.

And when presented with only two alternatives, we always choose one. Even if it doesn't make any sense. We choose one because we believe the other one is worse. It seldom occurs to us that there might be a dozen different alternatives.

While there are people who consider themselves philosophically liberal or conservative, very few of them actually work for the government or hold public office. Quite simply, if you're in a "conservative district" and want to win an election, you have to "be" a conservative.

Did you ever play intramural sports in high school? When I was in school, some of the boys would play intramural basketball at lunchtime. We had two teams: the shirts and the skins. The skins team played *sans* shirts.

We always wondered how the girl's teams handled that

but we never found out. The point is that each team competed and wanted to win, but in the end, we were all in the same school. It didn't really matter.

Congress is pretty much the same way. Republicans and Democrats, liberals and conservatives. And each team wants to win. In their case, winning means personal power like being majority leader or heading a powerful committee. Or getting legislation passed to benefit one of their special interests. But just like intramural sports, they're all in the same club. After work, they all go out drinking together.

It's just one big club, and you're not in it.

Because you're not on the team, all you can do is root for your favorite. Kind of like going to a baseball or football game. You have your pennant and team hat. And you root for the guys with the red jerseys, or the blue.

So we look at congress as being populated by good guys and bad guys. White hats and black hats. Red jerseys and blue jerseys. But it's just one big dog and pony show.

Every so many years we get tired of how things are going and decide to clean house. We throw one party out and put the other party in power. And we just *know* things are going to get better. They *have* to, because the guys with the white hats, with *our* jerseys, won!

But they don't. NOTHING EVER CHANGES.

Take a look at the last two administrations. Bush the conservative and Obama the liberal. Bush gave us the first stimulus, and Obama gave us the second. Bush ran up huge deficits and Obama ran up huge deficits. Bush gave us the Department of Homeland Security and Obama expanded it. Bush started wars in Afghanistan and Iraq and Obama continued them and started a couple more of his own.

Even Ronald Reagan, the conservative demi-god, *raised*

Taxes six times, grew the deficit and expanded the government. Can you think of one conservative who shrank the government by even one employee or one dollar? Can you think of one liberal who kept us out of war?

NOTHING EVER CHANGES.

No matter which team is in power, the government just keeps growing, taking more of our money, running up bigger deficits and taking more of our freedoms. And it doesn't matter how awful a program or policy is. It's there forever. Once you give up any part of your freedom to the government, you never get it back.

Myth #4: Government has a right to exist.

Government is a fiction. It's willed into existence, either from the top down or from the bottom up, as happened in our case. If government can be created from thin air, it can also be dissolved back into thin air. As Tomas Jefferson wrote in the Declaration of Independence, whenever a government becomes destructive of the rights of the citizens, they have a right to alter or abolish it. And why shouldn't we?

The government has no money of its own and it produces nothing. Everything it has and does it gets by taking it from the people.

To get a better idea of exactly what government is, consider this little analogy.

Let's say you work hard, holding down a full and part-time job. And your wife has a part-time job and does some volunteer work. Together you manage to bring home about five thousand dollars a month. In what spare time you have, you have to do the grocery shopping, cooking, cleaning and yard work, and help your children with their homework.

One evening after a long day, you finally sit down to watch an hour of television when the doorbell rings. It's a guy who introduces himself as an efficiency expert and professional home economist. He tells you that if you just give him a small portion of your income he'll relieve you of some of these tasks and do a better job than you can.

This sounds good to you so you agree to give the man a thousand dollars a month, for which he'll do the cleaning, yard work and grocery shopping, plus he'll take care of your savings and retirement planning. The rest of the money is yours for the rent, car payment and utilities and other expenses.

As time goes on you begin to notice that the grass isn't being cut as often as it used to be, there are cob webs in the corner of the living room and he's no longer buying the kinds of food you like. You complain and his response is that if you don't like the job he's doing you'll have to give him more money. You agree to start paying him two thousand dollars a month, but for the extra money, he'll also help your children with their lessons after school.

More time passes, your children's grades begin to slip and you discover he's been teaching them things you don't agree with. Further, the quality of the food he's been buying has been getting worse. He tells you he knows better how to teach your children than you do. After all, he's an expert and you're only a parent and therefore not qualified to teach your children. And the price of food has been going up, so if you want the kind of food you were used to, rather than paying him more money, you should just let him buy the groceries with your credit card. This doesn't make much sense to you, but now you're in pretty deep with this guy and you are locked into a contract.

Months go by and everything keeps getting worse. Then one day you open your statement from the bank and learn your credit card has been charged over its limit. You confront the man and he indignantly tells you he has expenses and if you want your credit card bill paid, you're just going to have to tighten your belt and be more frugal with the money he's been allotting you each month. "We all have to sacrifice, you know," he lectures you.

So eventually you get to the point where you feel you need to take charge of the situation. Among other things, you demand to see what he's done with your savings and retirement investments. He proudly tells you that on top of everything else he's done for you, he's made investments for you that are now worth nearly ten thousand dollars. You're impressed. Maybe this guy's better than you thought he was.

You ask for an accounting of your investments and the man brings you a box. The box is full of IOUs. "This isn't money!" you yell at him. "These are just a bunch of IOUs."

He explains that his expenses were greater than he thought they'd be and he had to borrow from your retirement fund, but the IOUs were just as good as money because they were backed up by money you'd be paying him in the future.

You realize that you've been bamboozled and you don't want him to work for you any longer. But he reminds you that you signed an iron-clad contract to make him your exclusive decision maker.

"What kind of extra expenses have you incurred?" you ask. He explains that he's been giving some of your money away to a couple of people who refused to be his friend unless he paid them. Further, he had to hire an assistant. He also bought a couple of guns. "Guns?" you ask. "Why do you need guns?" It turns out that the guy had been fooling around with the next door neighbor's wife and turning his children against him. And now the neighbor is threatening to kill him. "So I have to buy an alarm system for your house," he tells you. "I'm responsible for your security. Oh, and if your neighbor comes after me, I might need to call on your kids to help me fight him."

Exasperated, you finally tell him you're finished and you're no longer going to give him any of your money. He looks at you with cold steely eyes and says, "I don't think you want to do that. I can get very ugly."

Government is this guy. Only a lot bigger.

The government *supposedly* works for *us*. If it's not doing its job it deserves to be fired. We'll get into this further in Part Three.

In the next chapter, we'll look at many of the government's programs and policies in some detail, and you can ask yourself if they're helping you or hurting you.

But first, I'm going to give you a homework assignment. What follows is the Constitution of the United States. Your contract. *Take twenty minutes to read it*. Carefully. Make a note of what your contract *allows* the federal government to do.

We the People of the United

States, in Order to form a more perfect Union, establish Justice, insure domestic Tranquility, provide for the common defence, promote the general Welfare, and secure the Blessings of Liberty to ourselves and our Posterity, do ordain and establish this Constitution for the United States of America.

Article I

Section 1

All legislative Powers herein granted shall be vested in a Congress of the United States, which shall consist of a Senate and House of Representatives.

Section 2

1: The House of Representatives shall be composed of Members chosen every second Year by the People of the several States, and the Electors in each State shall have the Qualifications requisite for Electors of the most numerous Branch of the State Legislature.

2: No Person shall be a Representative who shall not have attained to the Age of twenty five Years, and been seven Years a Citizen of the United States, and who shall not, when elected, be an Inhabitant of that State in which he shall be chosen.

3: Representatives and direct Taxes shall be apportioned among the several States which may be included within this Union, according to their respective Numbers, which shall be determined by adding to the whole Number of free Persons, including those bound to Service for a Term of Years, and excluding Indians not taxed, three fifths of all other Persons. The actual Enumeration shall be made within three Years after the first Meeting of the Congress of the United States, and within every subsequent Term of ten Years, in such Manner as they shall by Law direct. The Number of Representatives shall not exceed one for every thirty Thousand, but each State shall have at Least one Representative; and until such enumeration shall be made, the State of New Hampshire shall be entitled to chuse three, Massachusetts eight, Rhode-Island and Providence Plantations one, Connecticut five, New-York six, New Jersey four, Pennsylvania eight, Delaware one, Maryland six, Virginia ten, North Carolina five, South Carolina five, and Georgia three.

4: When vacancies happen in the Representation from any State, the Executive Authority thereof shall issue Writs of Election to fill such Vacancies.

5: The House of Representatives shall chuse their Speaker and other Officers; and shall have the sole Power of Impeachment.

Section 3

1: The Senate of the United States shall be composed of two Senators from each State, chosen by the Legislature thereof, for six Years; and each Senator shall have one Vote.

2: Immediately after they shall be assembled in Consequence of the first Election, they shall be divided as equally as may be into three Classes. The Seats of the Senators of the first Class shall be vacated at the Expiration of the second Year, of the second Class at the Expiration of the fourth Year, and of the third Class at the Expiration of the sixth Year, so that one third may be chosen every second Year; and if Vacancies happen by Resignation, or otherwise, during the Recess of the Legislature of any State, the Executive thereof may make temporary Appointments until the next Meeting of the Legislature, which shall then fill such Vacancies.

3: No Person shall be a Senator who shall not have attained to the Age of thirty Years, and been nine Years a Citizen of the United States, and who shall not, when elected, be an Inhabitant of that State for which he shall be chosen.

4: The Vice President of the United States shall be President of the Senate, but shall have no Vote, unless they be equally divided.

5: The Senate shall chuse their other Officers, and also a President pro tempore, in the Absence of the Vice President, or when he shall exercise the Office of President of the United States.

6: The Senate shall have the sole Power to try all Impeachments. When sitting for that Purpose, they shall be on Oath or Affirmation. When the President of the United States is tried, the Chief Justice shall preside: And no Person shall be convicted without the Concurrence of two thirds of the Members present.

7: Judgment in Cases of impeachment shall not extend further than to removal from Office, and disqualification to hold and enjoy any Office of honor, Trust or Profit under the United States: but the Party convicted shall nevertheless be liable and subject to Indictment, Trial, Judgment and Punishment, according to Law.

Section 4

1: The Times, Places and Manner of holding Elections for Senators and Representatives, shall be prescribed in each State by the Legislature thereof; but the Congress may at any time by Law make or alter such Regulations, except as to the Places of chusing Senators.

2: The Congress shall assemble at least once in every Year, and such Meeting shall be on the first Monday in December, unless they shall by Law appoint a different Day.

Section 5

1: Each House shall be the Judge of the Elections, Returns and Qualifications of its own Members, and a Majority of each shall constitute a Quorum to do Business; but a smaller Number may adjourn from day to day, and may be authorized to compel the Attendance of absent Members, in such Manner, and under such Penalties as each House may provide.

2: Each House may determine the Rules of its Proceedings, punish its Members for disorderly Behaviour, and, with the Concurrence of two thirds, expel a Member.

3: Each House shall keep a Journal of its Proceedings, and from time to time publish the same, excepting such Parts as may in their Judgment require Secrecy; and the Yeas and Nays of the Members of either House on any question shall, at the Desire of one fifth of those Present, be entered on the Journal.

4: Neither House, during the Session of Congress, shall, without the Consent of the other, adjourn for more than three days, nor to any other Place than that in which the two Houses shall be sitting.

Section 6

1: The Senators and Representatives shall receive a Compensation for their Services, to be ascertained by Law, and paid out of the Treasury of the United States. They shall in all Cases, except Treason, Felony and Breach of the Peace, be privileged from Arrest during their Attendance at the Session of their respective Houses, and in going to and returning from the same; and for any Speech or Debate in either House, they shall not be questioned in any other Place.

2: No Senator or Representative shall, during the Time for which he was elected, be appointed to any civil Office under the Authority of the United States, which shall have been created, or the Emoluments whereof shall have been encreased during such time; and no Person holding any Office under the United States, shall be a Member of either House during his Continuance in Office.

Section 7

1: All Bills for raising Revenue shall originate in the House of Representatives; but the Senate may propose or concur with Amendments as on other Bills.

2: Every Bill which shall have passed the House of Representatives and the Senate, shall, before it become a Law, be presented to the President of the United States; If he approve he shall sign it, but if not he shall return it, with his Objections to that House in which it shall have originated, who shall enter the Objections at large on their Journal, and proceed to reconsider it. If after such Reconsideration two thirds of that House shall agree to pass the Bill, it shall be sent, together with the Objections, to the other House, by which it shall likewise be reconsidered, and if approved by two thirds of that House, it shall become a Law. But in all such Cases the Votes of both Houses shall be determined by yeas and Nays, and the Names of the Persons voting for and against the Bill shall be entered on the Journal of each House respectively. If any Bill shall not be returned by the President within ten Days (Sundays excepted) after it shall have been presented to him, the Same shall be a Law, in like Manner as if he had signed it, unless the Congress by their Adjournment prevent its Return, in which Case it shall not be a Law.

3: Every Order, Resolution, or Vote to which the Concurrence of the Senate and House of Representatives may be necessary (except on a question of Adjournment) shall be presented to the President of the United States; and before the Same shall take Effect, shall be approved by him, or being disapproved by him, shall be repassed by two thirds of the Senate and House of Representatives, according to the Rules and Limitations prescribed in the Case of a Bill.

Section 8

1: The Congress shall have Power To lay and collect Taxes, Duties, Imposts and Excises, to pay the Debts and provide for the common Defence and general Welfare of the United States; but all Duties, Imposts and Excises shall be uniform throughout the United States;
2: To borrow Money on the credit of the United States;
3: To regulate Commerce with foreign Nations, and among the several States, and with the Indian Tribes;
4: To establish an uniform Rule of Naturalization, and uniform Laws on the subject of Bankruptcies throughout the United States;
5: To coin Money, regulate the Value thereof, and of foreign Coin, and fix the Standard of Weights and Measures;
6: To provide for the Punishment of counterfeiting the Securities and current Coin of the United States;
7: To establish Post Offices and post Roads;
8: To promote the Progress of Science and useful Arts, by securing for limited Times to Authors and Inventors the exclusive Right to their respective Writings and Discoveries;
9: To constitute Tribunals inferior to the supreme Court;
10: To define and punish Piracies and Felonies committed on the high Seas, and Offences against the Law of Nations;
11: To declare War, grant Letters of Marque and Reprisal, and make Rules concerning Captures on Land and Water;
12: To raise and support Armies, but no Appropriation of Money to that Use shall be for a longer Term than two Years;
13: To provide and maintain a Navy;
14: To make Rules for the Government and Regulation of the land and naval Forces;
15: To provide for calling forth the Militia to execute the Laws of the Union, suppress Insurrections and repel Invasions;
16: To provide for organizing, arming, and disciplining, the Militia, and for governing such Part of them as may be employed in the Service of the United States, reserving to the States respectively, the Appointment of the Officers, and the Authority of training the Militia according to the discipline prescribed by Congress;

17: To exercise exclusive Legislation in all Cases whatsoever, over such District (not exceeding ten Miles square) as may, by Cession of particular States, and the Acceptance of Congress, become the Seat of the Government of the United States, and to exercise like Authority over all Places purchased by the Consent of the Legislature of the State in which the Same shall be, for the Erection of Forts, Magazines, Arsenals, dock-Yards, and other needful Buildings;--And
18: To make all Laws which shall be necessary and proper for carrying into Execution the foregoing Powers, and all other Powers vested by this Constitution in the Government of the United States, or in any Department or Officer thereof.

Section 9

1: The Migration or Importation of such Persons as any of the States now existing shall think proper to admit, shall not be prohibited by the Congress prior to the Year one thousand eight hundred and eight, but a Tax or duty may be imposed on such Importation, not exceeding ten dollars for each Person.
2: The Privilege of the Writ of Habeas Corpus shall not be suspended, unless when in Cases of Rebellion or Invasion the public Safety may require it.
3: No Bill of Attainder or ex post facto Law shall be passed.
4: No Capitation, or other direct, Tax shall be laid, unless in Proportion to the Census or Enumeration herein before directed to be taken.
5: No Tax or Duty shall be laid on Articles exported from any State.
6: No Preference shall be given by any Regulation of Commerce or Revenue to the Ports of one State over those of another: nor shall Vessels bound to, or from, one State, be obliged to enter, clear, or pay Duties in another.
7: No Money shall be drawn from the Treasury, but in Consequence of Appropriations made by Law; and a regular Statement and Account of the Receipts and Expenditures of all public Money shall be published from time to time.
8: No Title of Nobility shall be granted by the United States: And no Person holding any Office of Profit or Trust under them, shall, without the Consent of the Congress, accept of any present, Emolument, Office, or Title, of any kind whatever, from any King, Prince, or foreign State.

Section 10

1: No State shall enter into any Treaty, Alliance, or Confederation; grant Letters of Marque and Reprisal; coin Money; emit Bills of Credit; make any Thing but gold and silver Coin a Tender in Payment of Debts; pass any Bill of Attainder, ex post facto Law, or Law impairing the Obligation of Contracts, or grant any Title of Nobility.

2: No State shall, without the Consent of the Congress, lay any Imposts or Duties on Imports or Exports, except what may be absolutely necessary for executing it's inspection Laws: and the net Produce of all Duties and Imposts, laid by any State on Imports or Exports, shall be for the Use of the Treasury of the United States; and all such Laws shall be subject to the Revision and Controul of the Congress.

3: No State shall, without the Consent of Congress, lay any Duty of Tonnage, keep Troops, or Ships of War in time of Peace, enter into any Agreement or Compact with another State, or with a foreign Power, or engage in War, unless actually invaded, or in such imminent Danger as will not admit of delay.

Article II

Section 1

1: The executive Power shall be vested in a President of the United States of America. He shall hold his Office during the Term of four Years, and, together with the Vice President, chosen for the same Term, be elected, as follows

2: Each State shall appoint, in such Manner as the Legislature thereof may direct, a Number of Electors, equal to the whole Number of Senators and Representatives to which the State may be entitled in the Congress: but no Senator or Representative, or Person holding an Office of Trust or Profit under the United States, shall be appointed an Elector.

3: The Electors shall meet in their respective States, and vote by Ballot for two Persons, of whom one at least shall not be an Inhabitant of the same State with themselves. And they shall make a List of all the Persons voted for, and of the Number of Votes for each;

which List they shall sign and certify, and transmit sealed to the Seat of the Government of the United States, directed to the President of the Senate. The President of the Senate shall, in the Presence of the Senate and House of Representatives, open all the Certificates, and the Votes shall then be counted. The Person having the greatest Number of Votes shall be the President, if such Number be a Majority of the whole Number of Electors appointed; and if there be more than one who have such Majority, and have an equal Number of Votes, then the House of Representatives shall immediately chuse by Ballot one of them for President; and if no Person have a Majority, then from the five highest on the List the said House shall in like Manner chuse the President. But in chusing the President, the Votes shall be taken by States, the Representation from each State having one Vote; A quorum for this Purpose shall consist of a Member or Members from two thirds of the States, and a Majority of all the States shall be necessary to a Choice. In every Case, after the Choice of the President, the Person having the greatest Number of Votes of the Electors shall be the Vice President. But if there should remain two or more who have equal Votes, the Senate shall chuse from them by Ballot the Vice President.

4: The Congress may determine the Time of chusing the Electors, and the Day on which they shall give their Votes; which Day shall be the same throughout the United States.

5: No Person except a natural born Citizen, or a Citizen of the United States, at the time of the Adoption of this Constitution, shall be eligible to the Office of President; neither shall any Person be eligible to that Office who shall not have attained to the Age of thirty five Years, and been fourteen Years a Resident within the United States.

6: In Case of the Removal of the President from Office, or of his Death, Resignation, or Inability to discharge the Powers and Duties of the said Office, the Same shall devolve on the VicePresident, and the Congress may by Law provide for the Case of Removal, Death, Resignation or Inability, both of the President and Vice President, declaring what Officer shall then act as President, and such Officer shall act accordingly, until the Disability be removed, or a President shall be elected.

7: The President shall, at stated Times, receive for his Services, a Compensation, which shall neither be encreased nor diminished during the Period for which he shall have been elected, and he shall not receive within that Period any other Emolument from the United States, or any of them.

8: Before he enter on the Execution of his Office, he shall take the following Oath or Affirmation:--"I do solemnly swear (or affirm) that I will faithfully execute the Office of President of the United States, and

---

will to the best of my Ability, preserve, protect and defend the Constitution of the United States."

Section 2

1: The President shall be Commander in Chief of the Army and Navy of the United States, and of the Militia of the several States, when called into the actual Service of the United States; he may require the Opinion, in writing, of the principal Officer in each of the executive Departments, upon any Subject relating to the Duties of their respective Offices, and he shall have Power to grant Reprieves and Pardons for Offences against the United States, except in Cases of Impeachment.
2: He shall have Power, by and with the Advice and Consent of the Senate, to make Treaties, provided two thirds of the Senators present concur; and he shall nominate, and by and with the Advice and Consent of the Senate, shall appoint Ambassadors, other public Ministers and Consuls, Judges of the supreme Court, and all other Officers of the United States, whose Appointments are not herein otherwise provided for, and which shall be established by Law: but the Congress may by Law vest the Appointment of such inferior Officers, as they think proper, in the President alone, in the Courts of Law, or in the Heads of Departments.
3: The President shall have Power to fill up all Vacancies that may happen during the Recess of the Senate, by granting Commissions which shall expire at the End of their next Session.

Section 3

He shall from time to time give to the Congress Information of the State of the Union, and recommend to their Consideration such Measures as he shall judge necessary and expedient; he may, on extraordinary Occasions, convene both Houses, or either of them, and in Case of Disagreement between them, with Respect to the Time of Adjournment, he may adjourn them to such Time as he shall think proper; he shall receive Ambassadors and other public Ministers; he shall take Care that the Laws be faithfully executed, and shall Commission all the Officers of the United States.

Section 4

The President, Vice President and all civil Officers of the United States, shall be removed from Office on Impeachment for, and Conviction of, Treason, Bribery, or other high Crimes and Misdemeanors.

Article III

Section 1

The judicial Power of the United States, shall be vested in one supreme Court, and in such inferior Courts as the Congress may from time to time ordain and establish. The Judges, both of the supreme and inferior Courts, shall hold their Offices during good Behaviour, and shall, at stated Times, receive for their Services, a Compensation, which shall not be diminished during their Continuance in Office.

Section 2

1: The judicial Power shall extend to all Cases, in Law and Equity, arising under this Constitution, the Laws of the United States, and Treaties made, or which shall be made, under their Authority;--to all Cases affecting Ambassadors, other public Ministers and Consuls;--to all Cases of admiralty and maritime Jurisdiction;--to Controversies to which the United States shall be a Party;--to Controversies between two or more States;--between a State and Citizens of another State; --between Citizens of different States, --between Citizens of the same State claiming Lands under Grants of different States, and between a State, or the Citizens thereof, and foreign States, Citizens or Subjects.
2: In all Cases affecting Ambassadors, other public Ministers and Consuls, and those in which a State shall be Party, the supreme Court shall have original Jurisdiction. In all the other Cases before mentioned, the supreme Court shall have appellate Jurisdiction, both

as to Law and Fact, with such Exceptions, and under such Regulations as the Congress shall make.

3: The Trial of all Crimes, except in Cases of Impeachment, shall be by Jury; and such Trial shall be held in the State where the said Crimes shall have been committed; but when not committed within any State, the Trial shall be at such Place or Places as the Congress may by Law have directed.

Section 3

1: Treason against the United States, shall consist only in levying War against them, or in adhering to their Enemies, giving them Aid and Comfort. No Person shall be convicted of Treason unless on the Testimony of two Witnesses to the same overt Act, or on Confession in open Court.

2: The Congress shall have Power to declare the Punishment of Treason, but no Attainder of Treason shall work Corruption of Blood, or Forfeiture except during the Life of the Person attainted.

Article IV

Section 1

Full Faith and Credit shall be given in each State to the public Acts, Records, and judicial Proceedings of every other State. And the Congress may by general Laws prescribe the Manner in which such Acts, Records and Proceedings shall be proved, and the Effect thereof.

Section 2

1: The Citizens of each State shall be entitled to all Privileges and Immunities of Citizens in the several States.

2: A Person charged in any State with Treason, Felony, or other Crime, who shall flee from Justice, and be found in another State, shall on Demand of the executive Authority of the State from which he fled, be delivered up, to be removed to the State having Jurisdiction of the Crime.

3: No Person held to Service or Labour in one State, under the Laws thereof, escaping into another, shall, in Consequence of any Law or Regulation therein, be discharged from such Service or Labour, but shall be delivered up on Claim of the Party to whom such Service or Labour may be due.

Section 3

1: New States may be admitted by the Congress into this Union; but no new State shall be formed or erected within the Jurisdiction of any other State; nor any State be formed by the Junction of two or more States, or Parts of States, without the Consent of the Legislatures of the States concerned as well as of the Congress.

2: The Congress shall have Power to dispose of and make all needful Rules and Regulations respecting the Territory or other Property belonging to the United States; and nothing in this Constitution shall be so construed as to Prejudice any Claims of the United States, or of any particular State.

Section 4

The United States shall guarantee to every State in this Union a Republican Form of Government, and shall protect each of them against Invasion; and on Application of the Legislature, or of the Executive (when the Legislature cannot be convened) against domestic Violence.

Article V

The Congress, whenever two thirds of both Houses shall deem it necessary, shall propose **Amendments** to this Constitution, or, on the Application of the Legislatures of two thirds of the several States, shall call a Convention for proposing Amendments, which, in either Case, shall be valid to all Intents and Purposes, as Part of this Constitution, when ratified by the Legislatures of three fourths of the several States, or by Conventions in three fourths thereof, as the one or the other Mode of Ratification may be proposed by the Congress; Provided that no Amendment which may be made prior to the Year One thousand eight hundred and eight shall in any Manner affect the first and fourth Clauses in the Ninth Section of the first Article; and that no State, without its Consent, shall be deprived of its equal Suffrage in the Senate.

Article VI

1: All Debts contracted and Engagements entered into, before the Adoption of this Constitution, shall be as valid against the United States under this Constitution, as under the Confederation.
2: This Constitution, and the Laws of the United States which shall be made in Pursuance thereof; and all Treaties made, or which shall be made, under the Authority of the United States, shall be the supreme Law of the Land; and the Judges in every State shall be bound thereby, any Thing in the Constitution or Laws of any State to the Contrary notwithstanding.
3: The Senators and Representatives before mentioned, and the Members of the several State Legislatures, and all executive and judicial Officers, both of the United States and of the several States, shall be bound by Oath or Affirmation, to support this Constitution; but no religious Test shall ever be required as a Qualification to any Office or public Trust under the United States.

Article VII

The Ratification of the Conventions of nine States, shall be sufficient for the Establishment of this Constitution between the States so ratifying the Same.

Amendments -- The first ten are referred to as the Bill of Rights.

Article [I]

Congress shall make no law respecting an establishment of religion, or prohibiting the free exercise thereof; or abridging the freedom of speech, or of the press; or the right of the people peaceably to assemble, and to petition the Government for a redress of grievances.

Article [II]

A well regulated Militia, being necessary to the security of a free State, the right of the people to keep and bear Arms, shall not be infringed.

Article [III]

No Soldier shall, in time of peace be quartered in any house, without the consent of the Owner, nor in time of war, but in a manner to be prescribed by law.

Article [IV]

The right of the people to be secure in their persons, houses, papers, and effects, against unreasonable searches and seizures, shall not be violated, and no Warrants shall issue, but upon probable cause, supported by Oath or affirmation, and particularly describing the place to be searched, and the persons or things to be seized.

Article [V]

No person shall be held to answer for a capital, or otherwise infamous crime, unless on a presentment or indictment of a Grand Jury, except in cases arising in the land or naval forces, or in the Militia, when in actual service in time of War or public danger; nor shall any person be subject for the same offence to be twice put in jeopardy of life or limb; nor shall be compelled in any criminal case to be a witness against himself, nor be deprived of life, liberty, or property, without due process of law; nor shall private property be taken for public use, without just compensation.

Article [VI]

In all criminal prosecutions, the accused shall enjoy the right to a speedy and public trial, by an impartial jury of the State and district wherein the crime shall have been committed, which district shall have been previously ascertained by law, and to be informed of the nature and cause of the accusation; to be confronted with the witnesses against him; to have compulsory process for obtaining witnesses in his favor, and to have the Assistance of Counsel for his defence.

Article [VII]

In Suits at common law, where the value in controversy shall exceed twenty dollars, the right of trial by jury shall be preserved, and no fact tried by a jury, shall be otherwise re-examined in any Court of the United States, than according to the rules of the common law.

Article [VIII]

Excessive bail shall not be required, nor excessive fines imposed, nor cruel and unusual punishments inflicted.

Article [IX]

The enumeration in the **Constitution**, of certain rights, shall not be construed to deny or disparage others retained by the people.

Article [X]

The powers not delegated to the United States by the Constitution, nor prohibited by it to the States, are reserved to the States respectively, or to the people. The Judicial power of the United States shall not be construed to extend to any suit in law or equity, commenced or prosecuted against one of the United States by Citizens of another State, or by Citizens or Subjects of any Foreign State.

[Article XII]

The Electors shall meet in their respective states, and vote by ballot for President and Vice-President, one of whom, at least, shall not be an inhabitant of the same state with themselves; they shall name in their ballots the person voted for as President, and in distinct ballots the person voted for as Vice-President, and they shall make distinct lists of all persons voted for as President, and of all persons voted for as Vice-President, and of the number of votes for each, which lists they shall sign and certify, and transmit sealed to the seat of the government of the United States, directed to the President of the Senate;--The President of the Senate shall, in the presence of the Senate and House of Representatives, open all the certificates and the votes shall then be counted;--The person having the greatest number of votes for President, shall be the President, if such number be a majority of the whole number of Electors appointed; and if no person have such majority, then from the persons having the highest numbers not exceeding three on the list of those voted for as President, the House of Representatives shall choose immediately, by ballot, the President. But in choosing the President, the votes shall be taken by states, the representation from each state having one vote; a quorum for this purpose shall consist of a member or members from two-thirds of the states, and a majority of all the states shall be necessary to a choice. And if the House of Representatives shall not choose a President whenever the right of choice shall devolve upon them, before the fourth day of March next following, then the Vice-President shall act as President, as in the case of the death or other constitutional disability of the President. --The person having the greatest number of votes as Vice-President, shall be the Vice-President, if such number be a majority of the whole number of Electors appointed, and if no person have a majority, then from the two highest numbers on the list, the Senate shall choose the Vice-President; a quorum for the purpose shall consist of two-thirds of the whole number of Senators, and a majority of the whole number shall be necessary to a choice. But no person constitutionally ineligible to the office of President shall be eligible to that of Vice-President of the United States.

Article XIII

Neither slavery nor involuntary servitude, except as a punishment for crime whereof the party shall have been duly convicted, shall exist within the United States, or any place subject to their jurisdiction. Congress shall have power to enforce this article by appropriate legislation.

Article XIV

1: All persons born or naturalized in the United States, and subject to the jurisdiction thereof, are citizens of the United States and of the State wherein they reside. No State shall make or enforce any law which shall abridge the privileges or immunities of citizens of the United States; nor shall any State deprive any person of life, liberty, or property, without due process of law; nor deny to any person within its jurisdiction the equal protection of the laws.

2: Representatives shall be apportioned among the several States according to their respective numbers, counting the whole number of persons in each State, excluding Indians not taxed. But when the right to vote at any election for the choice of electors for President and Vice President of the United States, Representatives in Congress, the Executive and Judicial officers of a State, or the members of the Legislature thereof, is denied to any of the male inhabitants of such State, being twenty-one years of age, and citizens of the United States, or in any way abridged, except for participation in rebellion, or other crime, the basis of representation therein shall be reduced in the proportion which the number of such male citizens shall bear to the whole number of male citizens twenty-one years of age in such State.

3: No person shall be a Senator or Representative in Congress, or elector of President and Vice President, or hold any office, civil or military, under the United States, or under any State, who, having previously taken an oath, as a member of Congress, or as an officer of the United States, or as a member of any State legislature, or as an executive or judicial officer of any State, to support the Constitution of the United States, shall have engaged in insurrection or rebellion against the same, or given aid or comfort to the enemies thereof. But Congress may by a vote of two-thirds of each House, remove such disability.

4: The validity of the public debt of the United States, authorized by law, including debts incurred for payment of pensions and bounties for services in suppressing insurrection or rebellion, shall not be questioned. But neither the United States nor any State shall assume or pay any debt or obligation incurred in aid of insurrection or rebellion against the United States, or any claim for the loss or emancipation of any slave; but all such debts, obligations and claims shall be held illegal and void.

5: The Congress shall have power to enforce, by appropriate legislation, the provisions of this article.

Article XV

The right of citizens of the United States to vote shall not be denied or abridged by the United States or by any State on account of race, color, or previous condition of servitude.

The Congress shall have power to enforce this article by appropriate legislation.

Article XVI

The Congress shall have power to lay and collect taxes on incomes, from whatever source derived, without apportionment among the several States, and without regard to any census or enumeration.

[Article XVII]

1: The Senate of the United States shall be composed of two Senators from each State, elected by the people thereof, for six years; and each Senator shall have one vote. The electors in each State shall have the qualifications requisite for electors of the most numerous branch of the State legislatures.

2: When vacancies happen in the representation of any State in the Senate, the executive authority of such State shall issue writs of election to fill such vacancies: Provided, That the legislature of any State may empower the executive thereof to make temporary appointments until the people fill the vacancies by election as the legislature may direct.

3: This amendment shall not be so construed as to affect the election or term of any Senator chosen before it becomes valid as part of the Constitution.

Article [XVIII]

1: After one year from the ratification of this article the manufacture, sale, or transportation of intoxicating liquors within, the importation thereof into, or the exportation thereof from the United States and all territory subject to the jurisdiction thereof for beverage purposes is hereby prohibited.

2: The Congress and the several States shall have concurrent power to enforce this article by appropriate legislation.

3: This article shall be inoperative unless it shall have been ratified as an amendment to the Constitution by the legislatures of the several States, as provided in the Constitution, within seven years from the date of the submission hereof to the States by the Congress.

Article [XIX]

The right of citizens of the United States to vote shall not be denied or abridged by the United States or by any State on account of sex.
Congress shall have power to enforce this article by appropriate legislation.

Article [XX]

1: The terms of the President and Vice President shall end at noon on the 20th day of January, and the terms of Senators and Representatives at noon on the 3d day of January, of the years in which such terms would have ended if this article had not been ratified; and the terms of their successors shall then begin.
2: The Congress shall assemble at least once in every year, and such meeting shall begin at noon on the 3d day of January, unless they shall by law appoint a different day.
3: If, at the time fixed for the beginning of the term of the President, the President elect shall have died, the Vice President elect shall become President. If a President shall not have been chosen before the time fixed for the beginning of his term, or if the President elect shall have failed to qualify, then the Vice President elect shall act as President until a President shall have qualified; and the Congress may by law provide for the case wherein neither a President elect nor a Vice President elect shall have qualified, declaring who shall then act as President, or the manner in which one who is to act shall be selected, and such person shall act accordingly until a President or Vice President shall have qualified.
4: The Congress may by law provide for the case of the death of any of the persons from whom the House of Representatives may choose a President whenever the right of choice shall have devolved upon them, and for the case of the death of any of the persons from whom the Senate may choose a Vice President whenever the right of choice shall have devolved upon them.
5: Sections 1 and 2 shall take effect on the 15th day of October following the ratification of this article.
6: This article shall be inoperative unless it shall have been ratified as an amendment to the Constitution by the legislatures of three-fourths of the several States within seven years from the date of its submission.

Article [XXI]

1: The eighteenth article of amendment to the Constitution of the United States is hereby repealed.

2: The transportation or importation into any State, Territory, or possession of the United States for delivery or use therein of intoxicating liquors, in violation of the laws thereof, is hereby prohibited.

3: This article shall be inoperative unless it shall have been ratified as an amendment to the Constitution by conventions in the several States, as provided in the Constitution, within seven years from the date of the submission hereof to the States by the Congress.

Amendment XXII

1: No person shall be elected to the office of the President more than twice, and no person who has held the office of President, or acted as President, for more than two years of a term to which some other person was elected President shall be elected to the office of the President more than once. But this article shall not apply to any person holding the office of President when this article was proposed by the Congress, and shall not prevent any person who may be holding the office of President, or acting as President, during the term within which this article becomes operative from holding the office of President or acting as President during the remainder of such term.

2: This article shall be inoperative unless it shall have been ratified as an amendment to the Constitution by the legislatures of three-fourths of the several states within seven years from the date of its submission to the states by the Congress.

Amendment XXIII

1: The District constituting the seat of government of the United States shall appoint in such manner as the Congress may direct: A number of electors of President and Vice President equal to the whole number of Senators and Representatives in Congress to which the District would be entitled if it were a state, but in no event more than the least populous state; they shall be in addition to those appointed by the states, but they shall be considered, for the purposes of the election of President and Vice President, to be electors appointed by a state; and they shall meet in the District and perform such duties as provided by the twelfth article of amendment.

2: The Congress shall have power to enforce this article by appropriate legislation.

Amendment XXIV

1. The right of citizens of the United States to vote in any primary or other election for President or Vice President, for electors for President or Vice President, or for Senator or Representative in Congress, shall not be denied or abridged by the United States or any state by reason of failure to pay any poll tax or other tax.

2. The Congress shall have power to enforce this article by appropriate legislation.

Amendment XXV

1: In case of the removal of the President from office or of his death or resignation, the Vice President shall become President.

2: Whenever there is a vacancy in the office of the Vice President, the President shall nominate a Vice President who shall take office upon confirmation by a majority vote of both Houses of Congress.

3: Whenever the President transmits to the President pro tempore of the Senate and the Speaker of the House of Representatives his written declaration that he is unable to discharge the powers and duties of his office, and until he transmits to them a written declaration to the contrary, such powers and duties shall be discharged by the Vice President as Acting President.

4: Whenever the Vice President and a majority of either the principal officers of the executive departments or of such other body as Congress may by law provide, transmit to the President pro tempore of the Senate and the Speaker of the House of Representatives their written declaration that the President is unable to discharge the powers and duties of his office, the Vice President shall immediately assume the powers and duties of the office as Acting President.

Thereafter, when the President transmits to the President pro tempore of the Senate and the Speaker of the House of Representatives his written declaration that no inability exists, he shall resume the powers and duties of his office unless the Vice President and a majority of either the principal officers of the executive department or of such other body as Congress may by law provide, transmit within four days to the President pro tempore of the Senate and the Speaker of the House of Representatives their written declaration that the President is unable to discharge the powers and duties of his office. Thereupon Congress shall decide the issue, assembling within forty-eight hours for that purpose if not in session. If the Congress, within twenty-one days after receipt of the latter written declaration, or, if Congress is not in session, within twenty-one days after Congress is required to assemble, determines by two-thirds vote of both Houses that the President is unable to discharge the powers and duties of his office, the Vice President shall continue to discharge the same as Acting President; otherwise, the President shall resume the powers and duties of his office.

Amendment XXVI

1: The right of citizens of the United States, who are 18 years of age or older, to vote, shall not be denied or abridged by the United States or any state on account of age.
2: The Congress shall have the power to enforce this article by appropriate legislation.

Amendment XXVII

No law varying the compensation for the services of the Senators and Representatives shall take effect until an election of Representatives shall have intervened.

What Has the Government Done to Us?

We're going to start with the Federal Reserve, because it's the Fed that makes much if not most of the unlawful activities of the government possible. It's also the Fed that's responsible for the decline in the purchasing power of the dollar. When the Fed opened its doors for business, the dollar was worth a dollar. Today it's worth *four cents*. That's how much the dollar has been devalued sine 1913.

Along with that is the steady decline in Americans' standard of living. That's right, your standard of living has *fallen* every year since the Fed took control of the money supply.

How can that be, you ask. We have big screen TVs, satellite radio, really cool cars, computers and cell phones. That's the result of technology, and all those things have been invented and made affordable without (or in spite of) the government.

In real terms, the number of hours you need to work and the number of people in your family who have to work in order to pay for food, shelter, transportation, etc. have increased over the years, not decreased. The real measure of your standard of living is the amount of work it takes to maintain it.

As recently as the 1950s and '60s, the average head of the household worked nine to five with an hour off for lunch. In most cases, mom didn't work outside the home. Mortgages were short, never longer than twenty years. Almost no one had a credit card and cars were typically paid off in twenty-four to thirty-six months. Never longer. Other than a mortgage, many people lived debt-free. On one income!

I bought my first brand new car in 1966. It cost $2,700. And it was a pretty spiffy car. On my income of $150 a week I owned the car free and clear in eighteen months. That car would cost about $30,000 today. Try paying that off in eighteen months. People could afford things back then.

You might be inclined to think *everything* was less expensive back then, so it was easy to live on less money. But that's not so. Some things were *very* expensive. For example, in *today's* dollars, in 1965 a component stereo would have cost an easy two thousand dollars. A twenty-five inch color TV about thirty-five hundred dollars.

How has the Fed contributed to the decline in our standard of living, and our need to be in debt and stay in debt to maintain our level of comfort?

Earlier, I told you about the Rothschild banking dynasty in Europe, and how the Rothschilds and other powerful banking interests made numerous attempts to control the money supply in this country. In 1913 they finally did it. It started with an incredibly secret meeting on Jekyll Island off the coast of Georgia. It was there that the wealthiest and most powerful bankers in the world got together to draw up plans for what would become the Federal Reserve.

The chief architect of the Federal Reserve was Paul Warburg, a wealthy German banker and associate of the Rothschilds. And just as an aside, Paul Warburg was also the founder of the Council on Foreign Relations (CFR). The Rockefeller interests were also represented, along with J. P. Morgan, Jacob Schiff (who also personally financed the communist revolution in Russia) and others. So secret was their meeting that they all traveled to Jekyll Island on separate trains, and under assumed names.

The bill introducing the enabling legislation was introduced by Senator Nelson Aldridge, who represented the Rockefellers. The bill passed under rather questionable circumstances. But it did pass and the Fed was willed into being.

One thing the bankers knew was that Americans were very skeptical of central banks and the new central bank could be a hard sell to the public. So they gave it a safe and fuzzy name: The Federal Reserve. It sounded governmental and implied that there were actually assets. Reserve. Sounds like savings, doesn't it?

Here's what Mayer Rothschild figured out many years earlier: It's actually possible to create a loan that can never be repaid. And that's what central banking is all about.

All money in this country is *lent* into existence. Look at the bills in your pocket. They're Federal Reserve Notes. But what's a note? It's a debt instrument, like a car note or a mortgage note. You don't really have a dollar in your pocket. That reserve note means *you owe* the Fed a dollar. It's been *lent* to you. Every bit of cash you think you have is actually debt.

Our entire monetary system is debt based. Money is created when it's lent. When debt is repaid, the money disappears.

But here's where it gets *really* interesting. The Fed creates the principle, but not the interest. So the government, and by extension, you and I, have to keep borrowing more money so the Fed will create the interest for us to service our loan. So every year, we borrow more and pay more interest. We have to keep borrowing or the entire economy will implode. Because remember, when debt is repaid, the money disappears. And when I say "money" I'm referring to the funny money the Fed prints and lends to us. But in today's economy, that's what passes for money.

The same thing happens at your own bank. If you go into your bank and say you want to borrow thirty thousand dollars to buy a car, your bank *creates* that money out of thin air. It's just a bookkeeping entry, which is then transferred to your checking account. There's never any real money involved in the transaction. So how does your bank make money? It's called the fractional reserve system and it gets a bit complicated. So for the sake of brevity here's the easy version: The bank charges you interest on what it created out of thin air...and it gets to spend the interest.

It's almost as good as having a printing press in the basement.

The Fed operates essentially the same way. It lends *every dollar* into circulation -- at interest. And it gets to spend the interest. Billions and billions and billions. Great scam, huh?

But, as they say on TV at three in the morning, wait! There's more!

When the Fed was created, the bankers wanted some assurance that the interest on their loans would be paid. The government said, "No problem. We'll just tax their incomes and use that for payments on the debt." It required another constitutional amendment (the sixteenth), but they got it. And the IRS. The IRS is essentially the collection agency for the Fed. In fact there's a fair amount of evidence that it's not really a government agency, but that's a subject for another book.

It was easy for the citizens to accept the income tax, because in the beginning only the *very* rich paid any income tax and it was only about two percent. The personal deduction was twenty thousand dollars which was a hell of a lot of money back then.

Why was the income tax so low? The interest on the debt was minimal at that point because the Fed had just started lending money into existence. But in time, the lending would increase, the interest would increase, and so would taxes.

And to this day, the amount of money collected from personal income tax is about the same as the current interest on the debt. Your income taxes do nothing but pay the interest on debt, created out of thin air and lent into circulation. You get *no* government services from your income tax dollars

Here's a dirty little secret. If we put the Fed out of business, we can *eliminate* the income tax without losing a single government service.

We constantly hear about five-year plans and ten-year plans to pay down the debt. This nonsense has been going on for years. And have you noticed that none of these plans ever comes to fruition? We've never paid the debt down by a single dollar. *We just keep coming up with new plans.*

They have no intention of paying down the debt, because it can't be done. Everybody in Congress knows that and they're all lying.

Except Ron Paul. The only one in Congress with the courage to speak the truth.

What does all this have to do with the massive and unconstitutional government spending programs? The government couldn't pull it off if it had to tax you the full amount it was spending. So the government borrows from the Fed. At Interest. And *you* get to pay the interest.

For example, let's say George W. Bush went on television and said, "We want to invade Iraq, and it's going to cost every household in America about three thousand dollars." How many people do you think would have said, "Oh yeah! Go for it Prez. I'm all in!" Five, maybe six?

But wars aren't fought with taxes; they're fought with borrowed money. Money *you'll* be paying the interest on for *the rest of your life*. How do you feel about the Iraq war now? Or the war in Afghanistan. Or the War in Libya. Or the war in Pakistan. Or the war in Yemen. Or the war in Somalia. Oh yeah, we have lots of wars going on. But that's okay. We can just borrow the money.

So with this as a backdrop, let's look at some of the totally unconstitutional things the government has been doing, in most cases to our detriment, some with revenue raised from taxes and plenty of it borrowed -- at interest -- from the private monopoly bank that calls itself the Federal Reserve.

"The two enemies of the people are criminals and government, so let us tie the second down with the chains of the Constitution so the second will not become the legalized version of the first."

-- Thomas Jefferson

A Long List of Very Bad Things

As you read through this list of government programs, most federal, but a few local with federal oversight, ask yourself how these things got done before the government had its hands in them. Did children not eat lunch before the federal school lunch program? Were there no roads, trolleys, buses or trains before we had a dozen federal transportation agencies? Were farmers unable to grow food before there was an Agriculture Department? Were there not charities before the welfare programs?

My, my. How *did* we survive?

Washington, DC has become the world epicenter for bullshit and congress the world's biggest whorehouse. There's no war they won't engage us in, nor any ridiculous boondoggle they won't enact as long as the right lobbyist puts enough money in their campaign coffers. And this makes the typical congress person *worse* than a whore, because there are some things a whore *won't* do for money.

As you read through this list, remember that government is a fiction. It has no money other than what it takes from you in taxes, and it produces nothing on its own. It takes in a hundred dollars, squanders about half on itself, then gives the rest back to you *and tells you what to do with it.*

Does that sound like a good deal to *you*?

The Defense Department

Shortly before leaving office, President Eisenhower gave a speech in which he warned of the "military industrial complex". And boy, was he ever right.

The framers of our constitution gave the federal government the primary (but not sole) responsibility for the defense of the United States. And it didn't include a standing army. Our founders knew that if the government had a standing army, eventually it would want to use it. The founders figured if we were ever attacked the federal government could call up the state militias -- the citizen armies.

Today things are a bit more complicated and warfare more sophisticated. So perhaps a standing army makes more sense today.

For *defense*.

If the purpose of the military is to defend this country, what are we doing with our military personnel inside the borders of more than 130 different countries around the world? From whom are we defending ourselves? Is the *entire world* our enemy?

We have troops everywhere. Places like Jamaica. Do you feel threatened by Jamaica? I've been to Jamaica a couple of times and spent a lot of time hanging out with the locals. I found Jamaicans to be very lovely people. I listened to some reggae, ate some jerk chicken and, well okay, smoked a little ganja. Not once did I feel threatened.

Never did I overhear any plans to blow up Washington or New York. I don't know about you, but I don't think they're planning to do it. And even if they wanted to, I don't think they'd have enough money. It's a pretty poor country. So let's bring those troops home. One down, 129 to go.

Why do we have thousands of troops in Germany? I don't think they have any plans to attack us; they got their ass whipped in the last war. Or are we providing for *their* defense? If so, can't they do that themselves? Germany is a rich country. And the Germans are clever and innovative. They make good stuff. That's where all those Volkswagens and Audis come from. So they could make their own weapons and defend *themselves*, wouldn't you think? Okay, two down and 128 to go.

How about Korea? We went to war there sixty years ago *and never left*. Somebody needs to inform the Pentagon that the war's been over for a while and maybe it's time we came home. Hey, three down, 127 to go.

Here's an interesting one. We're also in Kyrgyzstan. And so are the Russians. We have a big presence in Kyrgyzstan. We use it as a staging area for troops and supplies on their way to another place we have no business being: Afghanistan. The Kyrgyz don't like us very much (But who does these days?) but they let us keep our base there because it's a poor country and we pay them a lot of money. So do the Russians. I don't think we need that one, either. Four down, 126 to go.

I could keep going down the list, but I think you get the point. If we brought our troops home from all the places we have no business being, we could save countless billions of dollars. All those soldiers we no longer need could go back home and get real jobs. And there'd be more real jobs because the cost savings would be so great that a lot of new private sector jobs would be created.

And why do we have so many enemies? If we were the great nation we seem to think we are, the whole world would be our friend. There are plenty of countries with little or no military, and no one attacks *them*. When's the last time you ever heard of anyone attacking Switzerland? Or Costa Rica? Right. And you know why? They don't piss anybody off. They're good neighbors. Maybe if we were a better neighbor more people would like us. Just a thought.

But the military and war are industries. A lot of people are getting rich. It's the military industrial complex President Eisenhower warned us about decades ago. The defense contractors love wars. They make stuff -- very expensive stuff -- it gets blown up and they get to make more. Such a deal.

A lot of our military adventures are sold to us as "humanitarian missions". Please. Why do we always take guns along on humanitarian missions? And somehow, many of our humanitarian missions end up with a lot of bloodshed. Hmmm. The military has two purposes: to destroy real estate and kill people. Humanitarian missions? Give me a break. Wouldn't the Red Cross be better at conducting humanitarian missions?

Another component of the military industrial complex is weapon sales to other countries. We make it possible for other countries to beat up on each other. As often as not, when a war breaks out somewhere, *both* countries are using weapons we sold them. And if any of the countries we sell weapons to fail to pay their bill (and some do) guess who picks up the tab for that? That's right, you and me. The companies who make and sell the weapons *always* get paid.

Had we concentrated on defending *our own* country over the past hundred years, rather than getting involved in foreign adventures all over the world, we could have saved *trillions* of dollars. And that's a lot of money.

Jeeeze. Why does one always need to preface remarks about this with the obligatory, "I'm not into conspiracy theories, but..."?

I'm not saying 911 was an inside job, but a lot of evidence points to it. On the other hand, it's just possible that nineteen devout Muslims, several of whom were partying it up in a strip club the night before, none of whom even knew how to fly a single-engine plane, expertly targeted the World Trade Center and the Pentagon.

But governments have been known to create what are called false-flag attacks on their own soil as an excuse to go to war. Even the Romans did it, so it's not exactly a new idea. The intentional sinking of the Lusitania got us into the war Woodrow Wilson wanted.

It's now an established fact that FDR knew well in advance that the Japanese were planning to bomb Pearl harbor. But the bombing of Pearl Harbor was really the second act of war since we were blocking their ports first. But that got us into the next big war.

Meanwhile, on the other side of the world, Hitler was setting the Reichstag (German Parliament building) on fire and blaming it on the communists as an excuse to go to war.

It was the Gulf of Tonkin incident that gave LBJ the green light to crank up the Vietnamese war. Years later it was discovered there was no such incident; the whole thing had been made up. But it lead to one long, nasty war.

And thanks to the Freedom of Information act, we now know about another false-flag operation. This one was stopped by President Kennedy at the last minute. The idea was to blow up commercial airliners, killing a lot of innocent Americans and accuse Castro's Cuba of the act. You can read about that one in official government documents.

The best way to get the populous to accept war is to convince the people that they were attacked *first*, and that's how most wars start. That said, I'm not saying nineteen devout Muslims didn't fly those planes into buildings. Maybe *this time* the government was telling the truth.

The War on Terror gives you a great opportunity to practice your new critical thinking skills. When a situation arises, the way the government deals with it should give you a good idea of what its real motives are. So let's look at what's happened since 911.

On the morning of 911, before the buildings had even fallen, the talking heads on TV were saying things like, "This has Osama bin Laden's DNA all over it." Where did that come from? Prior to that day he was a pretty obscure character. By the end of the day everybody *knew* it was him. And in pretty short order Bush was on television announcing that capturing bin Laden was priority numero uno and because we thought he was hiding in Afghanistan, that's where the military would be heading.

Never mind that bin Laden was a Saudi and all the alleged hijackers were Saudis. We were going to Afghanistan. This was an act of revenge and the beginning of the War on Terror, which we were told from the git-go would probably last *for the rest of our lives.*

So how do you find a man in hiding? Why, with tanks and warships, fighter jets and bombs. How else would you look for a missing person?

The sad truth is that we'd been planning to invade Afghanistan since May of that year. In fact we had our military on its way there before 911. It was reported in the mainstream press in at least a half dozen countries well before 911. It had everything to do with oil. Hey, there's a surprise.

Well, we've been in Afghanistan for a decade now, winning the minds and hearts of the people while we lob bombs at wedding parties, funerals and the like.

Meanwhile, back at the ranch, the White House, the Pentagon, the CIA and the defense contractors were cooking up the next war: Iraq. What threat did Iraq pose? Remember the weeks of propaganda? The weapons of mass destruction, the nuclear weapons program, Colin Powell at the UN showing *cartoon pictures* of supposed mobile chemical weapons factories?

If we fight them over there, we won't have to fight them here. So we were off on yet another war of questionable intent. And a new term was coined: preemptive war. Preemptive war is *starting* a war to *prevent* a war. Who thinks this stuff up? Put the book down for a minute and let that one sink in.

Anyway, we're still there, winning the minds and hearts of the Iraqi people. Not the million dead ones. But I'm sure the ones lucky enough to be alive and not poisoned by depleted uranium are *very* grateful for our presence. They'd better be because we have no plans to leave. Ever.

We're currently involved in preemptive wars, big and small, in Afghanistan, Iraq, Pakistan, Yemen, Somalia and Libya. Hey, you never know where a terrorist might be lurking.

But all this preemptive war began because we were looking for Osama bin Laden, the accused but never proven "mastermind" of 911. Check me on this if you want to. It'll take some Google patience and tenacity, but with enough effort you can learn that bin Laden has died four times. Once from kidney disease, twice by murder and the fourth time in a heroic assassination by Navy Seals.

I have no way of knowing for sure, but I believe the first death was the real one. Osama Bin Laden was very ill and on dialysis two or three times a week. On 911 he was already living on borrowed time. I always found it interesting that a severely ill man who needed dialysis was hiding in a cave in Afghanistan. Where did he plug in his dialysis machine?

The news of bin Laden's death from kidney failure and details of his funeral in December of 2001 was reported in *other* countries. This might explain why no one has seen or heard him since then. But later he arose from the dead to be murdered twice. At least one of the murders was reported on CNN and Fox News. And finally to be taken out in Hollywood style by Navy Seals, immediately after which all the supposed evidence was destroyed. If he was such a treasure trove of information, why wasn't he captured alive? Why wasn't he put on trial and if found guilty, executed? Why did the seals whisk his corpse into a helicopter to be dumped into the ocean? Where are the photographs? Where are the witnesses? Does *any* of this make any sense? One thing we do know: Bin Laden had more lives than a cat.

If we knew bin Laden was dead, why did we pretend he was alive? Because if you want to keep people afraid, a live terrorist is a lot more effective than a dead one. Governments lie.

Meanwhile, back in the homeland...

Because of Russia's matriarchal culture, the Soviet spy apparatus protected the "Motherland". Hitler watched over the patriarchal Germans with "Fatherland" security. I don't know. Maybe it's because of all our sexual confusion, but our government is protecting the "Homeland".

While the American military was all over Central Asia fighting them over there so we wouldn't have to fight them here, the Department of Homeland Security was getting into full gear to protect us from the Muslims hiding under every bed.

Time for a brief history lesson. Remember: If you don't know where you were you can't understand how you got where you are.

Those of us who've managed to find their way into geezerdom, as has your intrepid purveyor of truth, are old enough to remember the last great threat to Americans: the international communist conspiracy.

Here's how it went: The communists were "evil doers" who hated us because we were rich and free. They *hated* freedom and their goal was to enslave the world and convert it to communism. They had weapons of mass destruction and they intended to use them on us. At any moment. And they had managed to get into this country and were operating out of "sleeper cells" everywhere. They were infiltrating our businesses, our schools, even our churches. Frightened people were building bomb shelters in their basements or back yards.

But the most insidious of all the propaganda was what they did to school children. In addition to the obligatory fear mongering films shown in class, we had little exercises. I'm talking about elementary school children. The exercise was called "Duck and Cover". Here's how it went. An alarm would sound, similar to a fire alarm. When the children heard the alarm they had to quickly crawl under their desks and cover their heads.

Are you ready for this? Covering our heads would protect us from the atomic bombs the Russians were planning to drop on us. Of course, this was utter nonsense, but it sure kept the children afraid. Google "Duck and Cover". You can actually see some of the films.

Does any of this sound familiar? If not, try substituting Muslim for communist. Now does it sound familiar?

The truth, of course, is that the Russians had no intention of attacking us, but the fear was great for the military industrial complex. We built up a military as big as that of the rest of the world *combined*. Then one day, the Soviet empire collapsed and we were without an enemy. Can't have that, can we?

Enter al-Qaeda. And just like the communists, the al-Qaeda are out to destroy us. Turns out al-Qaeda was a creation of the CIA. It was a rag-tag outfit we used to fight the Russians

---

while *they* were wasting ten years in Afghanistan, after that same oil. The name al-Qaeda means "the list" or "the database". It was a list of people we could count on as insurgents against the Russians. Osama bin Laden was one of them and on our payroll for several years.

So just like the years of the Soviet menace, it's fear time again. This time on steroids. This time *everyone* is a suspect. And nowhere is safe. The government has information that al-Qaeda plans to attack shopping malls, train stations, sports stadiums, anywhere Americans like to go. We have yellow alerts, orange alerts. A color for every threat du jour.

Every week or so we're told there's a "credible threat" that terrorists are plotting something awful -- poisoning water supplies, blowing up power plants, always something awful. Something awful that never happens. But it's all fear, all the time. The fact is that you're far more likely to die in an automobile accident than from a terrorist attack, but you're not afraid to get in your car. Statistically, you're far more likely to win the lottery or get struck by lightening than to be killed in a terrorist attack. But the fear campaign is unrelenting.

We got the shoe bomber, as if anyone was going to blow up an airplane with a bomb in his shoe. I mean, really. It reminded me of Maxwell Smart. No, that was a shoe *phone*. But from that day forth, everyone who wanted to board an airplane (or for that matter even enter the local courthouse) had to take his shoes off. We're all suspects and are presumed guilty until we prove our innocence.

The last time my mother flew she was eighty-five years old and in a wheelchair. But she fit the terrorist profile. Hey, ya' never know. So the TSA mental giants yanked her out of her wheel chair and pulled off her shoes. Then they took her purse, dumped the contents on a table and rifled through them.

Eventually air travelers stopped whining about having to take their shoes off, so it was time to ratchet up security a notch. We got the underwear bomber. All he managed to do was set his pants on fire. But because someone could be hiding a bomb in his pants we now need to increase security even further. *And it just so happened that there was new technology ready to go*: The nudie scanners. We now all get a virtual strip search. And who owns the company that makes the scanners? One of them is Michael Chertoff who left his government post at the Department of Homeland Security to go into the nudie scanner business. How convenient. The government always takes care of its own.

Of course, if you object to the nudie scanner, you can opt to have one of the nice folks at the TSA shove his hand down your pants or up your skirt. And have them feel up your six year-old boy or teenage daughter.

Because we're all suspects and presumed guilty. Hey...IT'S-THE-PRICE-WE-ALL-PAY-FOR-FREEDOM, right?

But home-grown terrorists can be anywhere. So the nudie scanners are on their way to sporting events and elsewhere. They're already on some city streets in vans, peeking under the clothes of unsuspecting pedestrians.

But maybe, just maybe, the terrorists *aren't* planning to fly. Maybe they're sitting at home, planning their nefarious activities on their computer. Not to fear. We have Echelon and Carnivore, two nifty government programs that can read every one of your emails and monitor every one of your phone calls. Warrant? We don't need no stinkin' warrant. We're protecting the homeland. And the CIA and the NSA data mine Facebook all day long. They know everything *you've* been up to.

One of the newest programs is "See Something, Say Something". This program worked well for Hitler and Stalin, so it must be good. The idea is that you're supposed to pay close attention to what people are doing -- in essence, spy on your neighbors -- and if you see anything suspicious, you turn them in to the Feds.

And just who are suspicious people? According to internal DHS documents, among the most dangerous are Ron Paul Supporters, gun owners, gold enthusiasts and conservative political activists. Yes!

And what are suspicious activities? Objecting to things like the nudie scanners, using a video camera, talking to police officers, writing on a piece of paper, wearing a hoodie, driving a van and using a cell phone camera. I kid you not. It's right there in their promotional materials. Have the inmates taken over the asylum? Have you ever done any of those things? *You* could be turned in -- anonymously.

Critical thinking time again. Nineteen devout Muslims go drinking at a tittie bar, then the next morning they get on planes and fly them into the World Trade Center and the Pentagon. The mastermind was a Saudi man dying of kidney disease but supposedly hiding in a cave in Afghanistan. To find him and route out any other dangerous terrorists, we've spent ten years and a trillion dollars dropping bombs on innocent people in at least five countries. And at home we've torn the Bill of Rights into teeny tiny pieces. For our own safety.

In the meantime our southern border is wide open and if there really are any terrorists, they can just walk in with everybody else.

More and more it appears the War on Terror is really a war on the freedom and privacy of the American people. How much of this makes any sense to you? Is it possible, *just possible* that the government has a totally different agenda? Just asking.

"Nothing in politics ever happens by accident. If it happens, you can bet it was planned that way."

-- Franklin D. Roosevelt

The Food and Drug Administration

This is one of the myriad of federal agencies designed to protect us from ourselves. Were it not for the FDA we'd be consuming bad food and taking dangerous drugs. So we need geniuses in Washington to tell us what we're allowed to eat and how we're allowed to treat illnesses.

In the world headquarters of corruption, the FDA is perhaps the most corrupt agency in town. It regularly gives its approval to dangerous drugs with long lists of side effects sometimes worse than the illnesses they're supposed to be treating.

And it's no wonder. The drug industry has more money than God. And it's quite willing to spread a lot of it around to help finance your congresswhore's reelection campaign in exchange for favorable legislation, which is enforced by the FDA. And the FDA itself is just a revolving door. Top officials at the FDA come directly from the drug industry, where they then create rules favorable to the industry. Then they go back to work for the drug companies as lobbyists and pass more money around. Round and round they go.

Here's how it works, even on a state level. This example involving current establishment "conservative" darling, Texas Governor, Rick Perry, who signed an executive order *mandating* that *all* Texas sixth grade girls be immunized with the potentially dangerous drug Gardasil. Gardasil is made by Merck. *Coincidentally*, his former chief of staff was a lobbyist for Merck and his chief of staff's mother-in-law, Rep. Dianne White Delisi, was the state director of a group bankrolled by Merck to push legislatures across the country to enact legiislation mandating the Gardasil vaccine for preteen girls. Cost to Texas taxpayers: $60 million. Fortunately for 165,000 preteen girls in Texas, in a rare moment of conscience, the legislature overturned Perry's executive order.

Since we got the FDA to ensure our health and wellness,

83

half of the people in this country are overweight and degenerative disease has skyrocketed. Obese has become the new normal. And here's an interesting statistic. What do you think the three leading causes of death are? In order, heart disease, cancer and *drugs prescribed by your doctor*. Feeling protected yet? "Ask your doctor if Nosenseatall is right for you."

And speaking of cancer, it's been treated the same way for decades. Chemotherapy, radiation and surgery, or in simple English, poisoning, burning and cutting. Over the years many doctors and researchers have come up with innovative and less invasive ways to fight cancer, many of them as effective or more effective than the approved methods. These alternative therapies all have one thing in common: They're illegal.

The truth is that more people make a living from cancer than die of it. Cancer is a multi-billion dollar industry and the FDA intends to protect it.

While the FDA has seldom met a drug it didn't like, it's also seldom met a vitamin or herb it *did* like. Especially in the past few years, the FDA has launched a war on natural foods and alternative medicine. As I write this the FDA is raiding dairies (even Amish dairies) -- *with assault rifles drawn and aimed* -- for selling raw milk. Never mind that raw milk is more healthy than pasteurized and homogenized milk, or that until a few decades ago *everybody* drank raw milk and didn't die from it. These dairies are selling raw milk because there's a growing demand for it; they're simply providing a product people *want*. So we now have what amounts to the Gestapo raiding dairies.

Also as I write this, the FDA is threatening to confiscate something really dangerous: *walnuts*. The FDA has now classified walnuts as a drug.

The crime? The Diamond Food Company which is the biggest marketer of walnuts dared to say something *true* about its product. On its packaging and Web site, the company said, " The omega-3 fatty acids found in walnuts have been shown to have certain health benefits." Because the company made that simple and truthful claim, the product was now to be reclassified as a drug: *"Your walnut products are drugs...they may not legally be marketed ...in the United States without an approved new drug application."* The agency even threatened Diamond with "seizure" if it failed to comply. If you have walnuts in your pantry, I suggest you move them to the medicine cabinet where they really belong.

The FDA has been harassing sellers of other natural foods, as well. The FDA also hates pomegranates and green tea. But it loves just about anything marketed by the big corporate junk food producers. While no one's allowed to say that omega-3 fatty acids are good for you, potato chip manufacturers are allowed to call their products "heart healthy". Salty, high-fat potato chips -- heart healthy.

And thanks to the FDA's policies and protection of the drug industry, this country has the *highest drug prices in the world*. Indeed, many of the same drugs can be bought in Canada and elsewhere, sometimes for ninety percent less than what you're forced to pay in the land of the formerly free.

Remember: The government isn't here to protect your interests; it's here to protect its own interests and those of the big corporations that spread their money around to congress and the regulators.

Quite simply, we don't need the FDA. We got along just fine without it for many years. And without the FDA, we'd save billions in tax dollars and enjoy lower prices and more choices in the marketplace.

The War on Drugs

Have you noticed how much governments love war? They even declare war on ideas and inanimate objects. The War on Drugs dates back to the Nixon administration and it's been about as successful as the war on poverty. One thing I've observed over the years is that if you want more of something, just get the government to declare war on it.

There are a lot of reasons for the War on Drugs, but most of them have nothing to do with keeping you safe. Few people realize that until early in the twentieth century, *all* drugs were legal. Indeed, you could have sent your twelve year-old son to the drug store to bring back a package of opium for you. And you know what we didn't have? A drug problem. There were far fewer people using drugs when they were legal than there are now. In fact, in places where drugs have been decriminalized, drug use has gone down.

So why the war on drugs? It started with marijuana. To the best of my knowledge, no one has ever died from smoking marijuana. It's not even a drug. It's a weed, an herb. And apparently a lot of people think it's fun to smoke it.

But marijuana comes from hemp, which is a very beneficial plant with a wide variety of uses. It makes good paper and extremely high quality fibers for textiles. It's easy to grow and self renewing -- and it created serious competition to the cotton industry, which had a strong lobby. So a fear campaign was mounted to convince Americans that marijuana was a dangerous drug that caused violence, sexual promiscuity, insanity and death. Have you ever seen the movie, "Reefer Madness"? It was a movie produced back in the 1930s and secretly financed by the government. It was produced to create widespread fear of marijuana and was widely shown in movie theaters and schools.

In short, the prohibition of marijuana eliminated competition to the cotton industry -- and gave the government something new to regulate: things you might want to put in your mouth. So the list of prohibited drugs just kept growing. Any drug the FDA likes is a good drug, and any drug it doesn't is a bad drug.

Who else has benefited from the War on Drugs? Prisons. About half the population in prisons are non-violent, otherwise law-abiding citizens whose only crime was being caught with the wrong substance. What's little known is that most of the prisons in this country are now privately owned. Prisons have become an industry. A multi-billion dollar industry. And if you're going to invest a lot of money in a prison, you need to make sure it's well populated. So the prison industry also lobbies for strict drug laws.

And someone else who likes the drug laws: the police. First of all, busting a guy with a bag full of wacky weed is a lot easier than chasing down *real* criminals. But beyond that, if you get charged with *dealing* drugs (like selling to your friends) they get to take your property. If they find out you have a decent car that's paid for, and maybe a really nifty big screen TV, they just take them. All they have to do is *claim* you bought the stuff with drug proceeds and it becomes theirs. There's something in the Bill of Rights that says they can't do that, but who pays attention to that these days?

They don't even wait for you to be convicted to confiscate your property; they take it before you even go to court. So what happens if you're found not guilty, as some people are? Your property is gone. You see, they sell it and use the proceeds to buy new toys, like tasers.

The *producers and sellers* of illegal drugs also lobby for tough drug laws. They're making a ton of money and the last thing they want is for drugs to be made legal -- and cheap. And the big banks also support drug prohibition. Where do you think those drug producers and dealers launder their money?

But without the government preventing us from using all these drugs, the country would become overrun by drug-crazed zombies. Drugs would be everywhere. But drugs *are* everywhere. Any eighth grader in this country can by drugs within a block of his school. Or at the mall. Who are they trying to kid?

The problem isn't drugs; it's the prohibition of drugs. Early in the twentieth century, we went through alcohol prohibition. And what did we get? A black market in alcohol, ridiculously high prices and alcohol gangs and gang violence. If the government outlawed coffee tomorrow, coffee would cost fifty bucks a pound on the street, we'd have coffee gangs and coffee violence. Prohibition *never* works. Except for the enforcers and the black marketers.

So let's end the drug war and bring the drug troops home. We could save *billions* and let a lot of otherwise decent people out of prison.

I haven't done all the math but I think we've already completely eliminated the annual federal deficit. And hey, we're just getting started.

Hate Crimes

Since according to the Constitution, all crime enforcement is local, the federal government needed to invent some sort of new crime that states and municipalities seemed to be ignoring. *Thought crimes.* You can now be arrested and prosecuted for what you're thinking. So if you're arrested and tried for a so-called hate crime it's a *federal* matter. And if the Feds really want you it's almost impossible to win, no matter how innocent you are. They have all the money, all the lawyers and all the time.

But hate crimes are a very insidious thing and they're likely to lead us down a very slippery slope. "1984" meets "The Minority Report". You see, a hate crime isn't about what you did. It's about what you were *thinking* when you did it.

The truth is that state of mind seldom has anything to do with a criminal act. If a woman is raped, what matters is that she was raped, not what the guy was thinking at the time. Does his state of mind make the crime any better or worse? She was violated -- that's the crime.

But the hate crime legislation creates special classes of victims and special classes of people to be charged. Typically, if a gay man attacks a straight man, it's an assault, but if a straight man attacks a gay man, it's a hate crime. Gay men don't hate. If a white person attacks a black man, it's a hate crime because white people are racists. But if a black man attacks a white man, it's just an assault because black people aren't racists. If a Muslim attacks a Christian or a Jew, it's a hate crime (Or maybe even an act of mini terrorism). But if it's a Muslim who's attacked -- well he probably had it coming.

The thing is that at every opportunity, prosecutors look for opportunities to turn an act of violence into a hate crime any time the victim is a member of one of the privileged classes.

And we've already begun the slide down that slippery

slope. There have already been situations in which the hate crime didn't amount to much more than hurting someone's feelings or otherwise saying something offensive. Politically incorrect remarks.

The combination of hate crimes and political correctness is not a good one. Now we have to watch what we say to be sure nothing falls out of our mouth that might be *politically incorrect*. How many people in public life have lost their jobs just for saying something that offended *someone*?

It appears there's a committee of people working on a long list of things you're no longer *allowed* to say. A couple of years ago a member of the city council in Atlanta was forced to resign because he suggested the city be "niggardly" on current spending programs. Because niggardly sounded vaguely like the dreaded, awful "N" word, there was a big stink and the guy actually lost his job. By the way, niggardly is of Norse origin and means thrifty or stingy. But *somebody* was offended and that was enough.

What's next? Will Burger King have to stop selling the Whopper because it offends Italians? Will gyp become politically incorrect because it offends gypsies? Will Hispanics get pissed off and demand Spic & Span change its name?

Two things: No one can know for a fact what you were thinking when you committed a crime. And even if they could, it wouldn't matter. It's the *crime*, not what was on your mind. And second, politically correct speech, the step sister of hate crimes, is an dangerous step toward loss of freedom of speech. I have the right to say anything I want to. You have the right not to listen. I have the right to write and you have the right not to read.

Marriage

I'm old enough to remember when cohabiting was "living in sin". I knew people -- very nice people -- who were living in sin. I knew couples living in sin who were very much in love and treated each other like gold. And I knew people with the appropriate paperwork who were miserable, who were abusive and unfaithful to each other. And I used to wonder which ones were *really* married.

Marriage is one of the areas in which the church is in cahoots with the government. Why lack of government paperwork is any legitimate concern of the church I don't know. Through most of human history marriage has been a verbal commitment between two people, usually witnessed by family and friends. They *declared themselves* married. That was it. And if they decided to become unmarried at some time in the future, it was usually also a private matter.

Legal marriages are a fairly recent thing. In this country. It started with interracial marriages. If, for example, a white man wanted to marry a black woman, or an Indian man wanted to marry a white woman, the couple had to purchase a marriage license. They could get married (in most states) but only with special permission. If you wanted to marry someone with more or less melanin than you had, you needed permission from the government. Why was who you wanted to marry any business of the government? Of course it was none of the government's business, but when has that ever stopped it?

But every time you let the government crack open the door it won't be long before the door swings wide open. It wasn't long before *everybody* needed a permission slip from the government to sleep in the same bed.

It's easy and cheap to get married, but getting unmarried can cost you thousands. Or if you're rich, millions. Because a legal contract that required a few fees and a justice of the peace to commence, now takes lawyers and courts to dissolve. It was planned that way. Remember: lawyers grow up to become politicians.

If marriage is about love, commitment, respect, loyalty, protection and other warm and fuzzy things like that, what does a piece of paper have to do with it. And why still today do so many churches consider marriage *sans* government-issued papers living in sin? Is God looking down from the clouds, saying, "I see you're living in the same house. Do you have your papers?"

I can tell you one thing: Having possessed all the government-issued marriage paperwork, and having had my life ripped apart by divorce lawyers, you'll never see me standing in the marriage license line again.

In the past few years the government has involved itself even more in the business of marriage. Now the issue is gay marriage. The Republicans are running around waving the Defense of Marriage Act. Let's go back to the Constitution. Do you remember anything in it that said the federal government had any control over who marries who? Maybe the Republicans can find that clause, but I can't.

Why gay people would want to get married, I don't know. It sure hasn't worked out all that well for straight people. I have my own code of ethics and my own view of morality. And so do you. But I have no right to impose my beliefs on you, nor do you have the right to impose yours on me.

What anybody does in his home, and with whom, is no one's business but his and the person he's with, and certainly no business of the government.

Foreign Policy

America's foreign policy is like a web spun by a spider on bad drugs. It might make sense to people at the State Department, the Pentagon or the CIA, but not to normal people.

We have slimy spies, political operatives, assassins and other trouble makers in as many countries as we have military bases. We rig elections, kill heads of state, finance revolutions, bribe and threaten counties all over the world. We have allies (countries we've paid to be our friends) and enemies (countries we can't control).

We impose sanctions on and refuse to trade with countries we don't like. We did that to Iraq before Bush's war to liberate the Iraqis with our freedom bombs. But what...*what* did Iraq ever do to us? Nothing. It was just time for a "regime change". And *we're* the ones responsible for making those decisions. And it doesn't matter much whether we're dealing with a dictator or a popularly elected president.

For example, we liked Saddam Hussein for a long time. He was our guy. But at some point and for some reason, he managed to get on our shit list. So we killed him -- *on television*. Gaddafi used to be our guy, but now he's not. Time for another regime change. And Castro. We've hated Castro since the earth cooled. We act as though this harmless little Caribbean Island is some sort of threat and we boycott everything coming out of Cuba. And boycotts don't hurt the heads of state. Castro lives just fine. All our sanctions against Cuba do is hurt the Cuban people.

The countries we like best are the ones whose leaders dangle from strings controlled by puppet masters in Washington.

We're everywhere, in everybody's business. Especially in Central Asia. In that part of the world there probably haven't been four or five days when we *haven't* been dropping bombs on *somebody*. But that's okay. When *we* do it, it's *defensive*.

We're defending ourselves in *their countries*.

Part of it is just that weird government brand of English. When a plane is flown into the World Trade Center, it's an act of terror. When the CIA's secret army has people sitting at a computer console in Colorado guiding an armed drone into a residential neighborhood in Pakistan, blowing up women and children, it's a surgical strike. Innocent people? Oops. Our bad. Collateral damage. In the normal, sane world, family isn't collateral and death isn't damage. What it is, is murder.

In the first century of the American republic, we were the beacon to the world. The bright shining light of freedom. Everyone wanted to be like us. In recent decades the American empire has become the most hated and feared country on earth. Proud?

So what should our foreign policy be? It's not real complicated. The state shouldn't be allowed to do anything an individual isn't allowed to do. How popular would you be if you treated *your* neighbors the way the United States treats *its* neighbors?

If I were Secretary of State I could straighten things out in about twenty minutes.

Here's my plan:

1.   Bring the military home
2.   Bring the spies home
3.   Cut the puppet's strings
4.   Stop paying some people
5.   Stop punishing other people
6.   Extend the hand of friendship
7.   Trade fairly and honestly

And maybe bake a pie. But really, if we treated our neighbors around the world like we treat our neighbors up the street, the world would be our friends. Hell, they might even let us borrow their lawnmower.

Earlier I asked why no one has ever invaded Switzerland or Costa Rica (or a lot of other defenseless countries). They're good neighbors. No one hates them. What's so hard about that?

"In politics, what matters is not what the facts are; what matters is what people believe. Because people vote on the basis of what they believe and not what the facts are."

-- Thomas Sowell

Global Warming -- Oops, Climate Change

This might be the biggest fraud perpetrated on the people in many years. But there is so much governmental fraud these days that it's hard to figure out which is the biggest. Regardless, for all his lies and the millions of dollars he's made from them, Al Gore should be living in a place where they make license plates.

Remember: Whenever the government declares a crisis, take a hard look at its proposed solution. The solution will tell you what the real agenda is. In the case of global warming (or is it climate change?) the solution is even more government control, higher taxes, decreased freedom, and the government's favorite thing: sacrifice.

Sacrifice for us, not for them. Al Gore and the rest of the global warming hucksters fly everywhere in private jets, and ride everywhere in gas guzzling limousines while telling us we need to drive tin cans or take public transportation to save the planet. When Al Gore goes somewhere to speak, his driver leaves the engine running in the car to keep the temperature comfortable. And the utility bills in his enormous house are greater than many peoples' annual income. And his movie, "An Inconvenient Truth" was full of convenient nonsense.

Remember the beginning of the global warming scare? In just a few years, the oceans were going to rise, the poles were going to melt and temperatures everywhere were going to become unbearable.

Turns out they just cooked the statistical books. The earth has been *cooling* since 1999. The inconvenient truth to the global warming fear mongers is the earth heats and the earth cools. It always has. And the primary cause of global heating and cooling is the sun. Oh, and while the earth was warming -- slightly -- so was *every other planet in the solar system*. Last I looked there weren't any SUVs on Saturn.

And interestingly, the same pseudo scientists who were peddling the global warming crisis were warning of a coming ice age thirty years ago. They got it wrong last time, so why should we believe them this time?

So now everything's green. Green energy, green laundry detergent, you name it. It's all green. A lot of green in all these green projects. Windmills, electric cars and all kinds of things that don't work very well get huge government subsidies. Global warming has become just one more big industry feeding largely on the American taxpayer. And conveniently, a lot of people in the global warming movement are heavily invested in the subsidized solutions.

Oh, and reducing carbon dioxide. Ask the trees how they feel about that. Carbon dioxide is what they breathe. When they're healthy, they exhale oxygen, and that's what we breathe. As Ringo Starr once said, "Everything the government touches turns to crap." Tell the government to leave the planet alone.

"The principle, which is quite true in itself – that in the big lie there is always a certain force of credibility; because the broad masses of a nation ... more readily fall victims to the big lie than the small lie, since they themselves often tell small lies in little matters but would be ashamed to resort to large-scale falsehoods. It would never come into their heads to fabricate colossal untruths, and they would not believe that others could have the impudence to distort the truth so infamously."

Adolph Hitler -- *Mein Kampf*

But it gets worse. Yes!

You're gonna love this.

It may not rank as the most urgent reason to curb greenhouse gases, but reducing our emissions might just save humanity from a *pre-emptive alien attack*, claims a ridiculous new government report. Notice how it's not only the Pentagon that *starts* wars to *prevent* wars. Smart civilizations from other worlds apparently do the same thing.

Watching from afar, extraterrestrial beings might view changes in Earth's atmosphere as symptomatic of a civilisation growing out of control – and take drastic action to keep us from becoming a more serious threat, says the report.

"A preemptive strike would be particularly likely in the early phases of our expansion because a civilisation may become increasingly difficult to destroy as it continues to expand. Humanity may just now be entering the period in which its rapid civilizational expansion could be detected by an ETI because our expansion is changing the composition of the Earth's atmosphere, via greenhouse gas emissions," states this insane document.

So the latest reason for letting the government and the giant corporations control your life in the name of global warming is to protect us from an alien attack by beings from lands far away because they don't like what we've been (allegedly) doing to the earth.

"Green" aliens might object to the environmental damage humans have caused on Earth and wipe us out to save the planet. *"These scenarios give us reason to limit our growth and reduce our impact on global ecosystems. It would be particularly important for us to limit our emissions of greenhouse gases, since atmospheric composition can be observed from other planets,"* claims the report prepared for NASA's Planetary Science Division.

There's no nonsense our rulers won't stoop to for the purpose of increasing their power over us.

And we're *paying* for this crap.

The Department of Ejukashon

It was back in the 1960s that the federal government first cracked open the door to the control of education. It was a little program called "Federal Aid to Education". There was a lot of citizen resistance to this plan because of fears that federal money would end up being federal control. As always, the feds did everything they could to assure the people they had no desire to dictate any policies or curricula. As always, they lied.

We now have the Department of Education with an annual budget approaching a hundred billion dollars and a cost of regulatory compliance that brings the annual tax burden to nearly three hundred billion dollars a year.

Exactly what the Department of Education does besides pushing pencils and sliding mice isn't known. *It doesn't educate a single child.* That's a lot of money to spend on an education department that doesn't educate anybody. Mostly what the department does is make rules. Lots and lots of rules.

Since the first days of the American colonies, education was local. Children were taught by the church, by their parents or in neighborhood schools. They were taught by people who genuinely cared, and they learned. And as recently as the 1960s this is how children were schooled.

Because the schools were local and locally controlled, PTA meetings were well and regularly attended and parents were directly involved in what was being taught, and by whom. And if people with children moved to a new place, one of the considerations was the quality of the schools where they were going.

Back when parents had some control over their children's schools, this country was the best educated in the world. Today we're falling and falling fast, with third world countries sometimes providing better education. Reading, writing and math skills are abysmal. History is glossed over like it doesn't matter, presumably because it's old. A couple of years ago a survey of high school seniors in North Carolina discovered that twenty-five percent of them couldn't find the Atlantic Ocean on a map. This is astounding since North Carolina has a couple hundred miles of shoreline *on the Atlantic Ocean*. Yes, they lived right next to it but couldn't find it.

One of the impediments to learning is spending two or three hours a day riding a bus. Today it's believed that who a child sits next to is more important than what the child learns. So schools spend millions of dollars a year busing children across town. Millions of dollars that would be much better spent on things like, say, books.

The busing, of course, is to promote racial "diversity". While it's supposed to benefit black children, I'd think it would be insulting. What it's really implying is that a black child can't learn unless he's sitting next to a white child. I beg to differ, but in the city in which I grew up there were a couple of predominately black schools with *very* high academic achievement. Anyone who *wants* to learn *will* learn.

With federal control the schools have long lost the idea of the three R's. It's now all about socializing and political indoctrination. No longer is the goal of the schools to graduate well-educated and competent young adults; it's now about turning them into good, docile corporate citizens. Perhaps George Carlin summed it up best:

> *"They don't want well informed, well educated people... They want obedient workers, people who are just smart enough to run the machines and do the paperwork, but too dumb to rebel"*

Besides the curricula being dumbed down, discipline is totally out of control. Our public schools are plagued with sexual assaults, robbery, drug dealing and vandalism. Many schools have had to install metal detectors.

So every year the schools get worse, and every year they come up with some new scheme that's supposed to fix everything. I'll have to admit, though, that Bush II's No Child Left Behind program *has* changed things. Now *all* children are left behind.

And because the public schools have let our children down, colleges have had to lower their standards, too. Because so few high school graduates can do college-level work today. College has become little more than high school with six packs and ash trays. But it sure does cost a lot. After spending all that time and money, far too many of today's college graduates end up working in restaurants or selling phones at Verizon. It's sad.

The constitution gives the federal government *no* control over education. It's time we eliminate this unconstitutional (and therefore, illegal) department and return the money to the communities from which it was taken. Further, the government needs to get off the backs of private schools and home schoolers. Children educated in private schools and at home almost always outperform those in the government schools.

HIGHER Ejukashon

For years Americans have been conned into believing a decent career isn't possible without a four-year degree from college. I'm not against formal education, by any means. But "higher" education is for special training for such things as law, accounting, medicine and other professions.

For the people who attend college because someone told them they need to, or just because they want to spend an additional four years warming a chair, the prospects for a good job upon graduation are becoming bleak. Somewhere in the neighborhood of half of today's college graduates can't find good-paying work and end up moving back in with their parents. And more of them than you might imagine end up in jobs where their duties consist of asking questions. "Paper or plastic?" "Would you like fries with that?"

And unlike not all that long ago, when a student could only earn a degree in something useful, today you can graduate with a degree in almost anything you find amusing. If you're interested in seventeenth century Bolivian literature, you can be sure a college somewhere will grant you a degree in it. Although what good it will do you when you're asking your customer if he wants fries with that, I don't know.

One of my favorites is Women's Studies. I've been studying women all my life and still can't figure them out. How you can do it in four years, I don't know.

People who don't graduate from four-year colleges often do better than those who do. A good automobile technician can earn 80-100 thousand dollars a year. A year of training in a beauty or barber college can have a twenty year-old earning several hundred dollars a week.

And professions such as these offer excellent job security. People always need their cars repaired, and their hair keeps growing. These are *useful* jobs.

Another useful alternative would be to buy your son or daughter a franchised business. By the time his friends have graduated from college, your young entrepreneur would have a four-year head start on earnings and a lot learned in the real world. You could finance him or her with profits paid back to you at, say, ten percent a year. Your child owns his own business and you get paid back. Win/win.

There are also many good trade schools that can prepare a student for a good career in a year or two. Because they concentrate on preparing their students for specific careers without all the meaningless additional fluff forced on students in the four-year schools.

And here's where government meddling in yet another area in which it has no legal right to involve itself has made things even worse. Student loans. To encourage young people who won't necessarily benefit from a four-year college, the government got into the business of guaranteeing student loans. So now millions of young people leave school with massive debt -- before they even find a job.

Because the loans made financing higher education easier, colleges and universities have *drastically increased tuition* -- which, of course, just makes student loans all that much more necessary, increasing dependency on the government. Now a college graduate has to work many, many years *just to break even* on the cost of going to college.

And just like anything else the government makes a mess of, it's solution is to do *more* of it. With the stroke of a pen, the government has put itself in charge of *all* student loans. I can't find anywhere in the Constitution that says the government has a right to finance everyone's college education, can you?

Because the cost of college is so great, the prospects for good-paying jobs getting worse and the debt nearly impossible to repay, the student loan program could well be the next bubble to burst.

Another trillion dollar debt crisis.

And of course, as always, it's not the government financing college for millions of students -- it's you and me. Remember: The government has no money other than what it takes from the people -- or borrows at interest.

So just as you have to finance the government schooling of every kid in the neighborhood (through your property taxes), you're now financing their college education, as well. And when the student loan bubble bursts, guess who's going to be told to *sacrifice*?

The Economy and the "Stimulus"

The biggest problem with the American economy is that we don't make anything anymore. Or very little. It wasn't that many years ago that the whole world wanted American cars, furniture, cameras, radios and televisions, clothing, textiles, tires, steel and more. We now import most of these things. In fact, we import almost everything.

One thing third-world nations all have in common is that they don't make anything. With nothing of value to sell, there's no way to generate income. *You have to make things.* Today, other than government, *seventy percent* of our economy is people going to the mall. Consumer spending. You can't have a successful and healthy economy by shopping.

American business has moved off-shore for a variety of reasons, but perhaps the biggest is the cost of doing business here. In most cases the intolerably high cost of doing business in this country can be laid at the doorstep of the government. OSHA, the EPA, the EEOC, the Commerce Department and dozens of other onerous regulatory agencies have made doing business here non-competitive. We simply can no longer compete in the world marketplace.

Anytime a business wants to do something new or to expand its operations, it faces prolonged and costly forms, regulations, applications, court challenges and other government nightmares. As I write this, Boeing is trying to open a new manufacturing facility in South Carolina. It doesn't want to close its existing facilities; it wants to expand and open a new one. It's up to its eyeballs in a fight with the federal government. The government's position, pure and simple, is that it *won't allow* Boeing to open a plant in South Carolina because labor costs are lower there. Well, duh. Excuse me! Where does the federal government get the authority to tell you where you can locate your business?

Boeing would probably be better off doing what so many other companies have done and just go elsewhere. At some point it's just not worth the fight or the costs to do business here.

The cost of doing business in this country has become so great that if we *did* still make things here, most of them would be unaffordable *to Americans*. Were it not for imported goods, our standard of living would have fallen ever further. And even with lower priced foreign goods, in order to maintain our standard of living the average American family has had to resort to living the same way the government does: debt.

Today cars are typically financed for six or seven years, or leased. Homes are mortgaged for thirty years with little or down payment. Almost every retailer offers it's own credit card that can charged up in addition to our VISA and MasterCards. In many cases the payment terms exceed the useful life of the product purchased. People are putting their groceries on credit cards -- taking out a loan to by food. This is not good. We're drowning in debt.

And our debt further lowers our standard of living. Do a little math. How much of what you spend goes to interest to a bank? Mortgage, car payments, credit card interest, student loans. Add it up. You'll be amazed. Our debt service is so high and our savings so low that the average American is in trouble if he or she is out of work for even a few weeks. We're living on the edge.

Part of our problem isn't the fault of government. *It's us.* We've become narcissistic. It's all about what we *have*. Years ago if you saw someone drive by in a Mercedes-Benz, he was probably a rich man. Today if you have a job, you can probably get financed. Fancy restaurants are where we went for birthdays or anniversaries. Nowadays, they're where we go for dinner because we don't feel like cooking. Our children are wearing expensive designer clothing to school. We no longer go to get our hair cut; we blow a hundred bucks being pampered. We spend, spend, spend. Mostly for things we just don't need.

The day of reckoning has arrived. For us and for the

government. You can only use debt to support your lifestyle for so long. Eventually the bill comes due.

Whether it's personal, corporate or government debt, at the root of the evil is the Federal Reserve and the debt-based economy it's created. It was the Fed that was directly responsible for the housing bubble. Of course, the banks were complicit, as was Wall street. But they're all joined at the hip, each getting rich by creating debt so great it can never be repaid.

So the government to the rescue. Any time the government says it's going to fix something, watch out. Things are about to get worse.

We got our first stimulus under Bush II and the second under Obama. More than a trillion dollars. But where did this money come from? The friendly folks at the Federal Reserve just printed it, then lent it to us -- at interest.

If you were so deeply in debt that you couldn't make your payments anymore and were teetering on bankruptcy, would the smart thing to do be to borrow another thirty thousand dollars and buy a new car? Of course not. The smart thing would be to liquidate an asset or two and begin spending less until you were able to get your finances under control.

The federal government is about ten minutes away from bankruptcy and what the stimulus amounted to was spending a trillion dollars on new cars.

You can't get out of debt by incurring more debt.

Remember all the propaganda? Helping out Main Street instead of Wall Street? Shovel-ready projects? New jobs just waiting for stimulus funds? How much of it did *you* see?

There was so much stimulus money printed that had the government decided to give it to the *people*, every man, woman and child would have received $37,000.00. That's $148,000.00 for a family of four. If they were going to print it anyway, that's where it should have gone. It would have stimulated the economy. People would buy things, new businesses would be started and people hired, and people could have furthered their education without loans. There's no end to what could have been accomplished by that much money in the hands of *the people.*

I said "if they were going to print it anyway" because it is, in the end, just more debt. But if the government was going to incur more debt, why not spend the money where it could actually do some good?

So where *did* the money go? The government and the Fed have been quite secretive about where it all went -- always a bad sign. But we do know where a lot of it went. We bailed out banks (including *foreign* banks), Wall Street and big businesses. The government always takes care of its own, and you're not one of them.

So largely, the government bailed out the very people who caused the problem in the first place. As I wrote earlier, it's an exclusive club, and you're not in it.

Stimulus money got spread all around some of the biggest and most profitable corporations in America. Big business lined up for stimulus funds like pigs at the trough. Oink, oink, gimme more, gimme more.

Get caught with a couple of ounces of pot and do time; steal billions and get rewarded. Something is very, very wrong, wouldn't you say?

And we bailed out two car companies that should have gone bankrupt. The Chrysler bailout cost the taxpayers 1.3 billion dollars and the General Motors deal was so convoluted that no one will likely ever figure out how much was really lost. But it was a lot. What would have happened had these two car manufacturers gone bankrupt? Someone would have bought their assets and gone into business building better cars. Businesses go bankrupt sometimes. It's not the end of the world.

And where...*where* in the Constitution does it say the federal government can take money from the people by force and use it to buy businesses, which it then sells at a loss giving the final bill to those same taxpayers?

And typical of any government venture, part of the GM deal was the development of some stupid electric car that's *subsidized* to the tune of several thousand dollars per unit, and even with that, nobody wants one. It's even goofy-*looking*. By comparison the Toyota Prius is fine art. The combination of stupidity and corruption is very powerful.

Interestingly, Ford refused bailout money, is building excellent cars and doing great. I'd buy a Ford for that reason alone.

But these aren't the only places stimulus money went. Countless billions just went to the government. The problem is that anything useful or legal the government can do, has already been done many years ago. Now it's just silly things to waste money on. Or sometimes, very bad things. I'll give you just two examples, of thousands. One silly and one very bad.

There's a tiny town in Vermont with a border crossing to Quebec. There's a single customs agent on each side, because only about *two cars per hour* cross the border, and most of them are locals who cross to work or shop. Nearly six million dollars in stimulus money was earmarked to widen the border crossing to *eight lanes* and construct a new two-story building complete with a fitness center.

Sure, the project involved hiring a few temporary workers, but they aren't building anything anybody needs, so what's the point? It makes about as much sense as stimulating the economy by hiring people to dig holes and hiring other people to fill them in.

There are literally thousands of useless projects like this being done with stimulus money. Feeling stimulated yet? Or are you starting to feel something else?

In the category of very bad is this one. Stimulus money was spent to provide thousands of assault rifles to Mexican drug lords. I kid you not. This one even made the TV network news, and they're the *last people* to figure anything out. Undoubtedly, more stimulus money now will be needed to fight the Mexican drug lords and their new guns.

The bad stuff has hit the fan. The government is so far in debt that it's unlikely it'll ever see daylight again. And since in the end, it's you and I who pay all the government's bills, we're *all* in deep doo doo.

As well demonstrated over the past forty-five pages, if the government just got out of the business it has no business being in -- the things it has no constitutional authority to do -- we could balance the budget with no harm to anybody.

But what's congress doing? Proposing still more ridiculous spending programs and looking for new ways to extract more taxes from the people harmed by all the spending. The Democrats are unabashed spenders. More government! The Republicans *pretend* to want smaller government and to reign in spending. But listen carefully to what the Republicans say. They want to "slow the growth" of government. So the Democrats want to drive us off the cliff at a full gallop and the Republicans want to trot. But they both intend to drive us off the same cliff.

I haven't heard of any serious plans to reduce spending, have you? They're currently fighting over reducing the deficit by about two trillion dollars over ten years.. Reducing the deficit by that much over ten years (which they probably won't, anyway) still means *adding* about fifteen trillion to it. They're not reducing the deficit. They're merely reducing the *planned increase*. And wait until Obamacare kicks in. Whoa...watch out. If you think the debt is bad now, just wait.

The latest con is the proposed balanced budget amendment. First of all, constitutional amendments usually take years to take effect. They have to be approved by the state legislatures which is a pretty slow process. But beyond that, the whole idea is ludicrous. They're screaming that they want a balanced budget amendment because they *want* a balanced budget. Well, then, what's stopping them from just voting for one. *"Help me! I can't stop spending money. Pass a law to make me stop spending money! I can't help it. I'm sick. I'm addicted to spending money and need to go into deficit rehab!"* It's all just one big dog and pony show.

With one lone exception, every member of congress has violated his oath of office and should be impeached. Or worse. They're all members of the rich ruling class and our welfare isn't part of their agenda -- until election time. Then we matter for a few weeks.

If congress and the president *really* wanted to right the ship and get the debt under control, it could. No new programs. Eliminate all the unconstitutional programs. Eliminate all the programs that don't work (which is most of them). Bring the troops home from the 130 countries they have no place being. Hell, in a couple of years, we could eliminate the income tax and have a budget *surplus*. We could start making things in this country again and create millions of new jobs.

If you're one of those people who likes numbers, chew on this one. Since the stimulus this country *has lost an additional two million* jobs. If you want more of something don't put the government in charge.

Once government gets its claws into something, it never lets go.

"*See if the law benefits one citizen at the expense of another by doing what the citizen himself cannot do without committing a crime.*"

-- Frederic Bastiat

Immigration

Government usually gets what it wants. If it *wanted* to balance the budget, it would. If it *wanted* good schools, we'd have them. If it didn't *want* twelve million illegal aliens in this country, they wouldn't be here. I don't pretend to have the answers as to why the government wants them here, but it's obvious that it does.

Some people sneaking into this country is one thing, but twelve million is ridiculous. Interestingly, it's much more difficult to sneak into Mexico than it is to sneak into this country. The Mexicans protect their border.

Why is it obvious that the government wants them here? For a half century we've been *very* effectively protecting the Korean border. Hardly anybody crosses illegally. In either direction. We're pretty good at protecting borders when we want to be.

Beyond that, if the government really didn't want them here it wouldn't be so kind and generous. Illegals get drivers licenses, various kinds of welfare, their children get to attend school, and we now conveniently print everything in their language. We wouldn't want to inconvenience them by suggesting they learn English.

We're a nation of immigrants and I have no problem with someone wanting to come here and strive for a better life. And in some ways I can sympathize with people who sneak in. The legal immigration process is a typical government nightmare. And time-consuming. And expensive. I've been through it with somebody. It's not pretty.

I very much believe in a liberal immigration policy. I think we should welcome people of all nationalities and cultures to further enrich our salad bowl of a society. It's our blend of cultures that has made this a very interesting place to live.

But how about we did it this way? You can come to this country if you have an American citizen to sponsor you. And that person will be responsible for supporting you until you are self-supporting. If you don't speak English, you will enroll in a class to learn and be tested in six months. And further, if you run afoul of the law, your sponsor is liable.

I think this would give *good* people the opportunity to emigrate here and become productive citizens -- with no significant cost to the tax payers.

The government shouldn't make it so difficult to come here legally and so easy to just sneak in.

The Department of Agriculture

In the early days of farm subsidies, the program was sold to us as an attempt to save the family farm. Kind of like the stimulus helping Main Street and not Wall Street. Any time the government says it wants to help the little guy, watch out. When farm subsidies began, most farms in this country were family farms. Small businesses. And they did a fine job of providing quality food at affordable prices.

But as always, the real purpose of the farm subsidies was to promote something else. Today there are few family farms left. Indeed, most of the subsidies go to the big corporations, that need them least.

And in logic that only makes sense to government, most of the subsidies are for *not* growing food. They get paid for not producing anything. And it's billions of dollars. Such a deal. I'd love to get in on that.

There's an exception. If you produce ethanol you *do* get a subsidy for doing something. How did the ethanol producers get a subsidy? The short answer is that corrupt congressmen from states where the big corporate farms operate got the legislation through the House and Senate. So now the corporate farms get to produce ethanol, which would be a loser were it not for the subsidies -- and make money.

And whenever we go to the gas station ten percent of what goes into our tank is ethanol, which doesn't burn as efficiently as gasoline and therefore reduces our gas mileage. You get to subsidize rich corporations and put an inferior product in your gas tank. Sound like a good deal to you?

But it gets worse. Ethanol is made from corn. And taking millions of acres of corn for conversion to ethanol, has caused significant increases in the price of food. Corn is an ingredient in almost all processed food. Take a look at the ingredient list on the food in your pantry or refrigerator. There's corn something or other in almost everything. It's used as fiber, as a sweetener, as an oil and a lot of other things. Corn is a very versatile food crop. But now there's a shortage of it for food, and since the law of supply and demand hasn't been repealed (although Nixon tried in the 1970s) the price naturally goes up. And that means the price you pay for the finished product also goes up.

What's worse, and borderline criminal, is that food prices in poor countries have risen to the point where people, already marginal, can barely afford the most basic of food.

There are a lot of reasons for the recent significant rise in the price of food, but ethanol is a big one. And it's totally unnecessary. As always, the ethanol program is just one more way the government takes are of its own.

The Department of Agriculture is populated by bureaucrats who've never even seen a farm. Their job is just to make a lot of rules. Here's one. Food has to meet certain physical requirements. Like fruit has to be a certain minimum size. If it's smaller than what the law allows, *it's not food* and can't be sold. There was a situation in California a while back that would have been mind boggling to someone who didn't work for the government. A small farm wanted to take fruit (I believe it was peaches or plums, but I don't recall) that was smaller than the government mandated size and *donate* it to homeless shelters. A nice gesture, I think. They were prohibited from doing so, because since it was smaller than the mandated minimum it wasn't food and therefore couldn't be donated. Ponder that one for a minute.

But it gets worse. We now have genetically modified food (GMOs). In my slightly less than humble opinion the worst player in the genetically modified food industry is Monsanto, which is also a big recipient of government money. The real purpose for genetically modifying food isn't to make it taste better or be more nutritious; it's to make it cheaper and easier to produce and Transport. The problem is that it's all quite experimental and you're the guinea pig. No one knows what the long term effects of putting pig genes in tomatoes or apple genes in green beans (Or whatever they're doing; it's all quite secret) will have on human health. So far it's all *Frankenfood*.

Have you noticed in recent years how good the produce looks in the grocery store? Peaches, tomatoes and nectarines are huge and near perfect. They don't taste like anything but they sure do look good. They've all been genetically modified.

And the government says no one needs to tell you your food is being genetically modified. It may *look* like a peach but it's not *really* a peach. Not quite. The problem is we don't quite know what it is. Have you noticed how much better food you get from a farmers market tastes? It's *real* food.

Worse than that, genetically modified seeds won't reproduce. You can't take a seed from your tomato and grow new tomatoes. And if there's an organic farm near one of the big corporate farms producing GMO food and some of the GMO seeds blow onto the crops on the organic farm (which they do) they'll infect and ruin the natural crops.

Now Monsanto is producing genetically modified seeds programmed to cause the plant to die if you don't buy products from Monsanto to keep it alive. How nice.

A lot of countries are fighting the GMO food and some have outlawed it. But not here. Congress has been bought and paid for. And the government subsidizes this.

To help the big corporate farms monopolize the production of your food, the government is working overtime to make life somewhere between miserable and impossible for the small family farmers. Just as with any other industry, all that needs to be done to wipe out the little guy is to create regulations he can't possibly comply with.

For example, new proposed regulations will require anyone operating a tractor or other motorized equipment on a farm to have a commercial drivers license. A commercial drivers license to plow a field on your own property.

Commercial drivers operate things like tractor-trailers and earn good money. So the small family farmer will now need to hire and pay tractor-trailer drivers to plow their fields. And what do commercial drivers know about farming?

Do you see how everything the government does is to increase power and wealth at the top and diminish the independence and prosperity of ordinary Americans?

There's no constitutional provision for the federal government to control our food and the government needs to get out of that business. Food is a commodity and can be produced by small business people who care about what they do. Just like it's been done for centuries. When the government gets out of the farming business prices will likely go down and the quality will undoubtedly go up. And we'll save billions of dollars that are now being squandered.

Torture

This country's policy on torture is shameful. Waterboarding and many of the other techniques practiced by the military and the CIA are considered torture and are a violation of international law. But governments always have a dual morality. If *they* do it, it's bad, if *we* do it, it's good. When we do it, it's no longer torture. It's "enhanced interrogation techniques".

And just who is it we're torturing? Anybody; it doesn't matter much. Remember, we're in other people's countries fighting wars *we started*. To help round up "terrorists" we offer the locals rewards for capturing a suspected terrorist and delivering him to us. And if you're poor and the reward is big enough, almost anyone can start to look like a terrorist.

Is the suspected terrorist questioned, charged and if there appears to be credible evidence, put on trial? No. He's simply kidnapped, put on a plane and flown to one of our secret prisons somewhere in the world. And there he's kept, often for years, with no charges brought against him. Just tortured, hopefully until the pain and fear are so great that he'll eventually confess to anything his torturers want to hear, just to make it all stop.

This is how we obtain "confessions". Hitler and Stalin obtained confessions the same way. It worked very well for them, too. How much we've become like them.

How much pain would have to be inflicted on *you* until you'd say anything to make it stop?

Many of the kidnapped terrorist suspects eventually get released with no charges against them. But only after they've lived in inhuman conditions and repeatedly abused at the hands of their captors. By the time they're released their lives are in shambles. And often they're not returned home.

Instead we fly them to some other country and just drop them off. Strangers in a strange land. If they didn't hate us before they were kidnapped, they surely do by the time it's over.

The main reason these people are seldom charged with anything is that if they were, eventually they'd get their day in court where they would likely be acquitted. So they just sit in their horrible little cells and rot. Until it's time for the next round of torture.

There's another problem with torture. Every time the door to something is cracked open by government, eventually it gets opened wide. If it's okay to torture someone *over there*, how long will it be before it's done *over here*? Remember, these days a crime is anything the government says it is. They make it up as they go along. According to the Patriot Act, *almost anything* can be considered a terrorist act. Following the letter of the law, something as innocuous as lobbing a rock through a school house window can result in federal terrorism charges.

And just what is terrorism, anyway? If you're enjoying a family get-together in your back yard on a nice sunny afternoon, and all of a sudden a bomb is dropped on you from a drone flown remotely from the other side of the world, and your home is destroyed and half your family killed -- would you think of that as terrorism? When we do it, which we do every day, it's called a surgical strike.

Are there "terrorists" -- freedom fighters? Of course there are. Remember, we're in *their* countries fighting wars *we* started.

It's time the United States stops being the big bully on the playground, starts acting morally and ethnically and respecting the rights of everybody.

The TSA

The federal government's newest and fastest-growing behemoth is the TSA. Troglodytes with Surly Attitudes, Touch Somebody's Ass, Take Something Always. Indeed. TSA employees are like DMV employees with guns, they can't seem to resist getting their hands down your pants or inside your bra, and they steal. If there's something nice in your carry-on and no one's looking, when you land there's a distinct possibility it won't be there any more.

Tens of thousands of these employees cost us tens of billions of dollars a year. Their job is to consider every one of us a possible terrorist. More than 700 million people flew in this country last year. And *every one of them* was a suspect.

And the rules. The rules are insane. If you want to travel, first you have to run to the drug store and buy personal care products in teeny tiny sizes. Four ounces or less. Because an eight ounce bottle of shampoo is a potential weapon.

In fact almost anything can be considered a weapon. They seem to make these rules up as they go along, too. And we're all guilty until we can prove ourselves innocent.

Recently a man was arrested by the TSA *and jailed for four days*. When his backpack was scanned a bullet was discovered at the bottom. The man had recently returned from a hunting trip and the bullet was inadvertently left in the bag. Never mind that he had no gun and the worst he could have done with the bullet would have been to throw it at someone. Four days in jail. When arrested he was on his way home from a trip with his Boy Scout troop. Yeah, one scary dude.

So to keep ourselves safe we get to seen naked or have our stuff felt up. Because, hey, we could be hiding those bombs *anywhere*. Especially in places TSA employees like to look at or touch. Even small children and little old ladies.

What's interesting is that in countless tests, people have been able to get guns, knives, bomb parts and all kinds of things past the screeners. They miss that stuff, but they're vigilant about eight ounce bottles of mouthwash. Or bottled water. That's a potential weapon, too. Even if you bought it at the airport and it's still unopened.

What else can buy you trouble at the airport? Serious things like an offhand comment or the wrong look on your face. You have no freedom of speech at the airport. Come to think of it, you have *no* constitutional rights at the airport. If you want to fly somewhere, first you have to take a treacherous walk though Fedland. Enter at your own risk.

These days your time spent at the airport is likely longer than your flight. For example, you can drive from Pittsburgh to Cleveland in about two hours. Or you can fly in four hours.

It's all about fear. All fear, all the time. Fear, fear, fear. What if? Could happen.

Critical thinking time again. Statistically, the odds against your being the victim of a terrorist attack are far greater than the odds against your winning the lottery. And you know how much of a chance you have of doing that. Or being struck by lightening. In fact the odds of your being killed in your car -- *today* -- are greater than the odds you'll be killed in a terrorist attack *ever*. Why aren't you terrified to get in your car? The odds against your being killed in a terrorist attack are in the many millions to one.

But the government plays on a natural, but irrational fear. For some reason, people believe that if something highly unusual happens, it will happen again. The truth is that if something highly unusual happens, it probably *won't* happen again. Because it's highly unusual.

You wouldn't think so if you talked to the TSA. There are more than a *million* Americans on the No-Fly List. Apparently the government believes there are more than a million Americans who'd like nothing more than to blow up an airplane. Among the people on the No-Fly List are young children and dead people. Although I'm not sure the dead people feel very inconvenienced by it, I think the parent of a six year-old prohibited from flying would have a difficult time trying to explain why the family won't be flying to Disney World this year.

Airports reek of unpleasant, negative energy. Just *being* in the airport feels uncomfortable. Get used to it. This is what it's like anywhere the government controls *everything*.

And it's no longer just at the airport. The government is now putting its spy cameras *and nudie scanners* in city buses and in sports stadiums. Your facial expressions and eye movements are recorded and your image scanned with the government's face recognition software. Big Brother is watching *you*.

So how do we ensure our safety without the TSA? First, *allow* weapons on planes. Why should someone with a license to carry a gun not be allowed to carry it on an airplane? Assuming nineteen devout Muslims hung over from their previous night of partying at a tittie bar managed to bring down four commercial airliners with little knives bought from the office supply store, wouldn't a legally armed passenger or two have been able to stop them?

The free market can far more effectively screen passengers. The airlines have insurance policies and their insurance carriers will want to make sure the airline isn't taking any unnecessary risks. So they would come up with *sensible* ways of ensuring passenger safety. And because the airlines compete for your business, it would be in their best interest to provide for your safety with the least amount of hassle and discomfort.

Healthcare

Okay. Let me understand this. The government can't deliver the mail on time, it can't educate our children, it can't build sensible roads or provide public transportation, it can't make friends abroad without paying them, it can't balance its budget -- *or anything else*. And you think *this time* it will get it right.

Why anyone would want the government involved in something as personal as healthcare, I don't know.

We were told that Obamacare would reduce costs and increase choices. But *everything* the government does *increases* costs and *reduces* choices. There are no exceptions to this. Now that people have actually been allowed to read the bill no one in Congress apparently did, we learn that within five years the average American will be forced to spend an astounding *twenty percent* of his income on healthcare. That's one dollar out of five, for those of you educated in one of the government schools.

Obamacare ends medical privacy. Everything about your health will be available to anyone in the healthcare industry, the government, potential employers and presumably even credit rating agencies.

Further, Obamacare requires mountains of paperwork. The paperwork is necessary to prove your healthcare provider is following the mountain of new rules and regulations from Washington. Medical rules written by people who probably couldn't even apply a Band-Aid without reading the instructions.

And national healthcare will absolutely reduce your choices. All it has to do is refuse to pay for unapproved treatments or medications. These will certainly include any natural or "alternative" medicine. In fact, according to the legislation, the government will have the power to *force* medications and procedures on you. And possibly whether you get to live or have to sacrifice your life for the common good.

And if you think you can avoid the new healthcare monster by not buying the required insurance, Obamacare also provides for *sixteen thousand* new IRS agents to harass you and keep you in line.

And the healthcare legislation is a perfect example of the Democrats being what they are and the Republicans pretending to be something they're not. Typical of controversial legislation such as this, the Democrats supported the bill and the Republicans opposed it. But that was all just the Washington dog and pony show. Because the Republicans are all about big government and big spending, too. They merely pander to their voting base by *pretending* to be against the expansion of government.

In order for Obamacare to get through the Senate, they needed *just one* Republican vote. And the Republicans provided it at the last minute. That way they could have things both ways. They could get the legislation passed then go back to their districts and talk about how hard they tried to defeat it. "Dammit, dammit, dammit! We tried but just couldn't stop it."

With all the lobbying and the millions of dollars spread around the District of Criminals during the healthcare "debate", you can be sure all the big players have been well taken care of. The insurance companies, the big medical corporations, the drug companies the medical device makers and more will all profit handsomely from twenty percent of your income.

If you think medical care is impersonal and expensive now, just wait. No matter how expensive or bad it gets, your health will be in the hands of bureaucrats from now on. Once the government gets it claws in something, it never, never lets go.

Ad Hominem Attacks

Increasingly, this is how the government silences its critics. Instead of refuting the evidence, it simply impugns the intelligence or integrity of its critics. The most insidious, perhaps, is labeling someone a conspiracy theorist (or a conspiracy nut).

Okay, time for another critical thinking exercise. By definition, a conspiracy is two or more people planning to do something not in your best interest and not letting you in on the secret. Conspiracies are everywhere, big and small. It might be simple office politics, corporate price-fixing, an effort to unseat someone as president of the locals womens club, or children plotting something on the playground. Conspiracies are just part of life.

A little more critical thinking: If you get an idea that there might be a conspiracy, it's a conspiracy *theory*. If you're able to gather a little evidence, it's a conspiracy *possibility*. If you're able to assemble a lot of evidence, it becomes elevated to a conspiracy *probability*. And if the evidence is just too big and to credible to ignore, you have a conspiracy *fact*.

But no matter how much evidence someone has, it's always a conspiracy *theory* and he's always a conspiracy theorist (or a conspiracy nut). Not wanting to be labeled a nut, if you suspect foul play you always have to preface your remarks with something like, "I'm not into conspiracy theories, but..."

The fact is that governments -- all governments -- are conspiratorial by nature. They have to be. If they told you the truth about the things they do and why, you'd probably develop a serious attitude problem. Remember all those non-existent weapons of mass destruction that justified our attack on Iraq? That was a conspiracy. Of course, the official explanation was that *our entire intelligence apparatus* was mistaken. Oops. Our mistake.

But when confronted with very credible evidence of its complicity or involvement in the 911 attacks, Waco, the Oklahoma City bombing, rigged elections, an entirely too cozy relationship with Wall Street or a dozen other things, the government doesn't refute your evidence. It just calls you a nut. Case closed.

It's not just conspiracies; it's anything you think or say that differs from approved thinking or speech.

If you're ever critical of anything any black person might do -- or any individual or group of individuals -- you're a racist. To be critical of an action is to hate an entire group of people.

If you make fun of women, even jokingly, you're sexist. If you dare to, say, question the number of people killed in the holocaust you're not a historian; you're an anti-Semite. And if you see through the global warming hoax, you're a global warming *denier*.

And if you don't support special privileges for gays, you're a homophobe. This one's really interesting. You may have several gay friends and think they're fine people. You may not have a hateful bone in your body. You just have an issue with the politics. A phobia is an irrational fear of something and is considered an illness. So if you oppose anything political having to do with gays, it's not a philosophical difference of opinion; it's a mental illness: the irrational fear of gay people.

Being opposed to any official social policies makes you mentally unstable, and if you dare speak your mind, whatever comes out of your mouth becomes "hate speech". How many times have you heard the expression, "the politics of hate"? This is nothing less than an unofficial abridgment of free speech.

The next time you observe an ad hominem attack on someone, pay attention. He's probably on to something. If he weren't his arguments would just be shot down by logic or facts. When the government's actions, or those of it's circle of useful idiots, can't be defended, they just call you a name. Like third graders on the playground.

When you hear an ad hominem attack, what you're witnessing is someone who can't disprove or refute the information presented, so instead, he attacks the messenger. Whenever there's an attack on the messenger there's probably truth to the message.

Fascism

By every definition of the word, the United States has become a fascist empire. And fascism is more dangerous than communism because there are *multiple* enemies of your freedom. In the Soviet Union there was *one* enemy of freedom and everyone living there knew who it was. In a fascist state numerous powerful interests are in cahoots to take your liberty and property. Typically, the list includes organized religion, labor unions, big business, big banks and the government. They team up and cooperate for their share of the pie. Your pie.

But the principle players in a fascist state are the corporations, banks and government. And they're all so big it's difficult to determine which one's the dog and which one's the tail. But generally speaking, the corporations and banks run the show while the government keeps the citizens in line. Where are we now? You tell me. Does Washington run Wall Street or does Wall Street run Washington? Or are they partners? Hard to tell for sure.

I'm not into conspiracy theories, but...

This one's been the works for quite a number of years and they're deadly serious about it. Some of those not so nice people who'd love nothing more than to get their claws on your freedom and property, figure why stop at one country when they can control the entire planet?

So, quietly, behind the scenes, they're working on it. NGOs, so-called free trade agreements, the United Nations, the World Bank, the Trilateral Commission, the Bilderberg Group and others. All quietly leading us in that direction. If they're able to pull this one off, it'll no longer matter where you live, because wherever you are, you'll wish you were somewhere else.

The NWO plans are to turn the world into a big feudal society. And if you think you're going to be anything other than a serf, you're sadly mistaken.

They're accomplishing this, mainly through treaties. Treaties entered into unconstitutionally. These are agreements the president unilaterally enters into by executive order, while the congress just whistles and goes on its merry way. How convenient. If you saw some of the treaties this country has entered into in recent years, you wouldn't be able to sleep at night. Here's an especially scary one. Google "Agenda 21" and see what you get.

Slowly, insidiously, one step at a time, our sovereignty is being chipped away. Snip, snip, snip.

Who Writes All These Bills, Anyway?

You can read the entire Constitution in about twenty minutes. But to read a typical bill introduced into the House or Senate could take a month. Some of them run into the thousands of pages. Do you think anybody in the congress writes any of these? *Hell, they don't even read them.* They're written by lawyers in the employ of the various special interests who paid to get your Congresswhore elected. He just presents it.

And they all have warm and fuzzy titles. "A Bill to End Poverty and Create Eternal and Universal Happiness". Like that. As a general rule, the nicer the title sounds the more dangerous the legislation is. Most bills state their purpose with specifics, but end with a pretty spooky generality: "...and other purposes". I don't know about you, but I'd be interested in knowing what those other purposes are.

Ethanol bills are written by the ethanol industry. Banking bills are written by members of the banking industry. Federally mandated child safety seats are the result of bills written by people who make child safety seats. If you want to sell more of something, just make it a law. Same with the automobile industry. For years the automobile manufacturers offered various kinds of safety features as available options. They weren't selling as many of them as they would like to have. No problem. Make it a law and suddenly what was an individual choice becomes something you have to buy. Cha ching. That's how it works.

So bills written by special interests are voted on by people who don't read them. But they have hours, or sometimes days of debate on them. Debate? How can you debate what you haven't even read? Well, they don't actually debate the substance, wisdom or legality of the bill. They just spew forth clichés, slogans, talking points and other meaningless rhetoric to create the illusion that they're passionate, one way or the other, about the Bill-to-Take-More-of-Your-Freedom-Away du jour. Great way to run a country, huh?

If you want a real eye-opening experience, watch C-Span for a week. Watch all these clowns fighting for face time on C-Span's cameras. Truth be told, most of them know exactly how they're going to vote from the git go. The "debate" is just a big dog and pony show to make it look like they're thinking and they care.

You want to change things really fast? Three things:

1. Demand that all bills have to be written by a member of the House or Senate.

2. Demand that each one is read by every Senator or Representative before debate or voting.

3. Post the bills on the Internet the same day they're introduced.

What do you think? Sound reasonable?

The Patriot Act

The mother of all bills to be voted on without being read is the Patriot Act. Not only was it not read, but no one was even *permitted* to read it prior to voting.

This should raise a lot of questions. Questions like, who wrote it and when (since it had already been written *prior* to 911)? *Why* was no one permitted to read it? And of course, what was in it?

Remember: How a government deals with a situation or reacts to a crisis will always tell you what its *true* motives are. In the case of the Patriot act it would be useful to review a little bit of history again.

After Hitler's *false flag attack* on the German Reichstag, a bill was presented to the legislature. It was called the Enabling Act. The Enabling Act gave Hitler the legal authority for every one of his dastardly deeds, and its passage was rushed through the German legislature the same way the Patriot Act was rammed through Congress. More troubling is that some of the language in the Patriot Act was taken *verbatim* from Hitler's Enabling Act.

Let's imagine *you* were in charge of things in Washington, DC after the events of 911. What would you likely do? Here are a few logical possibilities. Maybe you'd conduct a real and thorough investigation to determine who actually perpetrated the attacks, where they came from, who financed them and what their motives were. Then you'd probably want to know how they were able to get past a zillion layers of defense and security and catch the entire apparatus off guard.

You might also want to learn how jet fuel, which is kerosene and burns at 575 degrees, could melt enough steel in a 110 story building to make it collapse and crumble into its own footprint. My barbeque grill burns *hotter* than jet fuel. Why doesn't *it* melt and collapse? I don't know why, but I'd like to.

You might even want to know why the forty-seven story World Trade Center Number Seven collapsed *the exact same way* even though nothing hit it.

After doing a thorough investigation and getting answers that seemed to make sense, you'd probably present your findings to Congress and the American people and propose ways to deal with the perpetrators and make similar future events far more difficult to accomplish.

I'm not suggesting the answers; I'm merely posing the questions and a logical response to what happened on 911. Your job is to do a little critical thinking and perhaps come up with your own list of questions and possible solutions.

We're still in critical thinking mode here. Only this time you're not in charge of things. Now you're an outside observer. You might want to ask yourself how and why, within an hour or two of the attacks, talking heads were all over the TV networks telling us that Osama bin Laden was behind the attacks, and he was roaming around Afghanistan, moving from mud huts to caves, presumably dragging his dialysis machine and a very long extension cord behind him. Amazing! A crime solved before an investigation.

Not only did we *immediately* know Osama bin Laden was the "mastermind" of the attacks, but we also knew the identities of all nineteen of the alleged highjackers and had their names -- and pictures -- on CNN within about twenty-four hours.

You might want to know how two days previous, no one in the federal security apparatus had the foggiest idea something like this could happen, then immediately figured out who did it and how. I'd also like to know how they so quickly learned the identities of the alleged highjackers and obtained their pictures, since *not one* of their names appeared on the passenger manifests of any of the involved flights.

I don't have the answers. I only have the questions.

We're still doing critical thinking. Now you're back in charge of things. Given a long list of questions that need answers, would your *first* action be to heavily borrow from Hitler's Enabling Act and ram it though Congress without permitting anyone to read it? *Would it?*

After the fact, we now know what was in the Patriot act. And it's not pretty. The Bill of Rights attached to the Constitution was written to protect us from our own government. It said the government wasn't allowed to spy on us, punish us for saying what was on our mind, try us repeatedly for the same crime, imprison us without evidence and formal charges against us, engage in torture, invade our privacy (our person and property) and more.

The Patriot Act violates *every one* of the Bill of Rights. No wonder no one was allowed to read it.

The federal government, specifically the legislative branch (the President) now has as much power over us as Hitler and Stalin did over the Germans and Russians. Are you feeling safe now? Are the terrorists a small gang of disgruntled Central Asians or the entire population of this country? Judging from its reaction to 911, it appears the government has decided *we're* the enemy.

Right now you might be thinking, "I still have my rights. I'm still free. I'm not doing anything wrong so I have nothing to worry about." To the extent that you haven't been arrested, you're right. But *everything* you do is monitored *in real time*. All your bank transactions, your shopping activities, where you go in your car, what you're doing on the street, what you're saying on the phone and writing in emails, and more. *You have no privacy.* What did you do or say today that might retroactively become a crime next week?

And of course, if you object to having your property confiscated at the airport or make an unflattering remark, you can be arrested for the federal crime of bad attitude.

Yeah, we're still free. As long as we don't violate any of the scores of new rules that make us an enemy of the state merely by exercising our liberty.

And remember that Hitler an Stalin didn't come down on their citizens with an iron fist overnight. It was a little at a time until eventually there was no freedom left. Snip, snip. Clip, clip. A little here and a little there until there until freedom was only something seen in the rear view mirror. Are you feeling a little snipping? A little clipping?

The Patriot Act is how bad things can get when members of the House and Senate vote on bills they haven't read. So perhaps I should repeat my solution to such madness, proposed in the pervious segment:

1. Demand that all bills have to be written by a member of the House or Senate.

2. Demand that each one is read by every Senator or Representative before debate or voting.

3. Post the bills on the Internet the same day they're introduced.

In the Case of the Patriot Act, I might propose a fourth useful rule:

4. Repeal bad legislation.

There are literally millions of federal crimes. You likely commit a dozen or two of them every day. The Patriot Act added layers of new ones. Laws you're not even aware of. Yet.

Consider this: Over this past summer *children* all over the country have been arrested for selling lemonade in their front yard without a permit (a permission slip *purchased* from the government).

When *this* is a crime, *anything* is a crime. Government on every level is totally out of control and needs to be reigned in *now*. NOW.

Lobbyists

I have no problem with lobbyists. It's called freedom of speech and the right to the redress of grievances. Anybody should have the right to try to influence the legislature.

The problem is all the whores. 535 of them. Alright, maybe 534 of them. Hundreds of millions of dollars are spread around in their attempts to buy votes. Why? Because the votes are for sale. If they weren't the lobbyists wouldn't be there spreading all that money around. No matter the financial condition of someone entering Congress, by the time he leaves he's usually quite wealthy. I don't think it came from his salary, do you?

2011's lobbyists of the year had to be drug, medical and insurance industries, making sure everything they wanted got into the monstrous Obamacare legislation. Millions and millions were spread all over town. You can be assured that nothing bad will happen to any of them.

So again, the problem isn't lobbyists. They have a right to suggest, complain or anything else they'd like to do. The problem is a legislature populated by members of the Anything-For-a-Dollar Club. Washington, DC was built on a swamp, but it's become a cesspool.

Elections

Elections in this country have become a farce.

If someone wins with, say, sixty percent of the vote he's declared to have a "mandate". But the reality is that he was probably the first choice of six or seven percent of the people. First of all, only about half the eligible voters actually do, so that takes his sixty percent down to about thirty. And during the primary election, he was probably one of several different candidates, each winning a few percent of the vote. And an even smaller percentage of people vote in primary elections. In reality, the winner was the first choice of very few people.

Beyond that, a lot of elections are rigged. They always have been. Years ago, Lyndon Johnson won a congressional election by vote fraud. And Ron Paul lost one the same way. And who alive back then can forget the 1960 presidential election which was decided by a few thousand dead people voting in Cook County, Illinois? Elections used to be rigged by ballot stuffing, losing ballots or deliberate miscounts. Today any eighth grader can hack a voting machine.

As Josef Stalin famously said, *"It's not who votes that counts; it's who counts the votes."*

Politics is a dirty game. Most politicians will step deeply into any kind of slime for the opportunity to be of service to the people.

And how much do you *really* know about the people you vote for? What important things do you know of their past? Have you looked into their voting records? Have you checked to see who's financing their campaigns?

Knowing who finances the campaigns tells you what they're really going to do, and for whom, if elected.

Where do you go for such information? Your local

newspaper, radio and television stations are of no help. Typically, they just regurgitate the candidates' sound bites and slogans. More about that coming up.

Learning anything of substance about a candidate for office requires some work, because nobody really *wants* you to know anything. You need to spend a lot of time on the Net. And not at FoxNews.com or CNN.com.

Most of what you learn (or think you learn) about candidates for office comes from one source: television. It's either debates or commercials.

The debates are a joke. They're not debates. A real debate would concentrate on one issue and the candidates would spend an hour *debating* it. What passes for debates are all the candidates lined up on a stage with the media's favorites positioned front and center and the ones they don't like over on the edges.

The debates are moderated by some TV news talking head with good hair. His job is to lob softball questions at the favored candidates and ridiculous questions to the guys over on the edges. They don't even all get the same questions. And since the candidates know, or at least have a very good idea what the questions are going to be, they have plenty of time to rehearse their one-minute sound bite answers.

When the debate is over, just to make sure the viewers understood what was important and what wasn't, the TV useful idiots are there to help us. Several of them sit around a table and discuss which one looked "presidential", which one was the most polished and poised and if any of them failed to wear the obligatory American flag lapel pin. Sometimes they'll comment on a candidate's tie, too. Just to show they were paying attention.

At the end, they show us the *science*. A pollster with a *very carefully* selected group of people to interview. People whose answers were predictable even before the debate began.

And surprise, surprise -- the focus group responses always favor the establishment's favored candidates.

Anyone who would prefer a more honest competition should tune into "American Idol" instead.

Beyond the silliness passing as debates, what television gives us is commercials. Political commercials that grow in frequency until we feel like shooting our TV. These are thirty or sixty-second commercials produced by some of the top advertising agencies in the country. The commercials are carefully written, then tested to make sure they're believable (yes). If they're not they're rewritten.

The commercials aren't about what the candidate is; they're about what you can be made to believe. And what can you learn about a candidate in sixty seconds, anyway. Exactly what they want you to learn: nothing. What we *do* learn is that every candidate grew up as the son or daughter of a coal miner, has three beautiful children, is an outsider who will go to Washington and single handedly rid the city of corruption and loves America.

Political candidates are marketed like cars, soft drinks and the drug that cures Restless Leg Syndrome. So we go to the polls and vote for the one we hate less than the other guy.

And it doesn't matter very much who wins because they never do what they promised they would in the campaigns and therefore, nothing important ever changes. Obama has broken virtually every one of his campaign promises. And just to be fair, so did Bush. They all do. All a campaign promise is, is telling you what you want to hear. If they thought voting would *really* change anything it wouldn't be legal.

The News Media

The only free press we still have is on the Internet and if the powers that be have their say about it, that free press will become a thing of the past one day soon.

Newspapers are quickly losing their readership, first because they're mostly fluff. The days of the crusading reporter are long gone. And second, because you actually have to *read* a newspaper. The same is true of the once great weekly news magazines, for the same two reasons. They're headed the same way as the newspapers. So most Americans get their news from television or talk radio.

You have to understand that TV news isn't really news. It just looks like news. It's all show business. I'd hazard a guess that the TV news channels spend more money on fancy sets and special effects than they do on investigative journalism. And your favorite news person belongs to a union: AFTRA, the American Federation of Radio and Television Artists. The radio and television actors union. If they were truly *journalists* they wouldn't have to belong to an actors union, would they?

The primary qualifications to be a TV news anchor are, if you're a man, a good voice and the ability to tie a Windsor knot. If you're a woman, strikingly good looks, big hair and two other things. Oh, and in both cases, the ability to read things you don't really understand from a teleprompter.

To become a trusted news anchor, you have to know how to look in the camera and read your script with great confidence. As if you investigated it all yourself. The fact is that hardly anybody in television news investigates anything. For example more than eighty percent of stories about the economy are read *verbatim* from government news releases. How's that for getting to the bottom of things?

And the biggest TV news channels have been caught with their journalistic pants down on more than one occasion. Until exposed it was a common practice to pretend to be standing in a place where news was happening, such as the White House. Turned out the reporter was just standing in front of a green screen in the studio.

And then there was CNN's reporting live from Baghdad in the early days of the war in Iraq. Turns out they were just standing in the next room with palm trees and other props. If you can't even believe they're where they say they are, how can you believe anything else they have to say?

How did it come to be this way? One of the very few things the government has ever deregulated is the broadcasting industry. And it had its reasons, as always. Several years ago the FCC decided a company could own as many radio and television stations as it could buy up. The result is that about five huge corporations now own nearly every radio and television station and cable network in the country. In some markets one company can have a monopoly, owning every station in town. And because broadcasting stations owe their very existence to the government through licensing, they certainly wouldn't want to do anything to ruffle the feathers of the good folks at the FCC who make their billions of dollars in profits possible.

Remember the section on fascism? The huge broad-casting conglomerates are now part of the game.

And the government also enforces. Several years ago the CIA *bragged* that it had an agent in nearly every major newsroom in the country. Just to make sure you're getting the truth, of course. Step out of line and the feds can pull the plug on your thousand radio and television stations.

> *"The Central Intelligence Agency owns everyone of any significance in the major media."* -- William Colby, former CIA Director

"There is quite an incredible spread of relationships. You don't need to manipulate Time magazine, for example, because there are [Central Intelligence] Agency people at the management level." -- William B. Bader, former CIA intelligence officer, briefing members of the Senate Intelligence Committee

Conservatives are constantly whining about the "liberal" news media and consider Fox News a gift from God himself. There's no "liberal bias" at the TV news networks. There's pro government bias. The presentation differs because each network wants to capture certain viewers. Consequently, liberals tend to like MSNBC while conservative prefer Fox News. I don't think anyone watches CNN anymore. I expect they're prime-time news anchors are getting beaten in the ratings by the local weatherman on channel nine.

Regardless of which news program you prefer to watch, the actual content varies little. In fact sometimes you can surf back and forth and hear a story read on each network *in the exact same words*. It's the presentation. One screams against the conservatives while the other rails against the liberals. But they both sure do like government. And the multi-national corporations and banks. That they all have that in common. The real agenda isn't liberal or conservative; it's to keep you as *un*informed as possible.

Talk radio is a different story. It tends to be very conservative. Not by design, but because liberal talk show hosts have seldom been able to capture and keep an audience. And talk radio tends to be local. There are some syndicated talk shows, but for the most part the broadcasting day is dominated by local personalities.

The biggest exception to this is a guy named Rush Limbaugh. And I gotta tell you, I think Rush Limbaugh is very talented. As a former radio personality, I respect his talent. He has an engaging personality, a powerful delivery, a quick wit and a sophisticated sense of humor.

But when it comes to credibility, Mr. Limbaugh scores something close to zero. He's never met a Democrat he liked, nor a Republican he didn't. Every problem in the world has been caused by the LIBERALS! He's just the Republican Party's daily mouthpiece. And no matter what the burning issue of the day is, you know exactly what he's going to say about it before he even opens his mouth. If I'm in the car when Limbaugh comes on, I'll listen for ten or fifteen minutes then quickly switch to Sirius-XM for some music. There's only so much of him I can take.

And talk radio is full of Rush Limbaugh wannabes. Partisan fear-mongering neocons. But somehow or other, a few intelligent, principled and knowledgeable libertarians have managed to find a place in talk radio. They speak very thoughtfully about the issues of the day and are a breath of fresh air.

The point is that you're not going to learn much from radio or television, although talk radio can be quite entertaining. The only place left is the Internet. Enjoy it while you can, because the government is working overtime to figure out how to ruin that, too.

Group Think

The government and its useful idiots in the TV newsrooms have been fairly effective in putting us all into neat little categories. In market research it's referred to as group consensus. It's very advantageous to the powers that be for us to think as groups, rather than as individuals. It's part of its divide and conquer strategy.

If the government can divide us all into groups it becomes easier to pit one group against the other with each group lobbying for special treatment and favors from the whores on the Potomac.

Liberals have a long list of things they're *all* supposed to believe. Conservatives, too. The same is true of rich people, poor people, black people, white people, old people and young people. We think like our group. Our tribe.

Polls are part of the group think nonsense, too. Hardly a day goes by without the TV talking heads talking about the latest poll. Because we've gotten very comfortable settling into our little group, it's important that our opinions don't drift too far astray. Polls remind us of how we should be thinking. "Sixty-seven percent of conservatives say…" Well, there you go. That's what you need to think. You certainly wouldn't want to be in the minority.

Presidential polls are particularly insidious. First of all they're usually skewed. You can get any answer you want if you ask the question just right. And second, sadly, we tend to vote for the candidate we think can win. Like it's a horse race or something. How many times have you heard someone say, "I really like this guy but I don't think he'll win, so I'm voting for the other guy." We all want to vote for the winner.

It's called group think. The problem is that we're all individuals and therefore should *think* like individuals. Why can't a conservative agree with a liberal about some things? One of the greatest insults a black person can receive from another black person is that he thinks or acts white. What in the world is thinking white? Do all white people think the same? Are all black people *supposed* to? And can't a rich person and a poor person share some of the same ideas? And of course, we all know Hispanics are all the same, right?

The government pits one group against another and generates fear. The best example of that today is the fear campaign against Muslims. There are a billion of them and we never know which one of them wants to blow us up. I hate to be the one to burst that little bubble, but Muslims are individuals, too. Just like you and me.

But if the government can gin up enough fear in one group about another, it can win our allegiance and *protect* us. And that's exactly where it wants us.

Critical thinking time again. Start thinking *for yourself*. Regardless of what people around you might think. And start finding things you have *in common* with other people. When you think like your group you see the world through the tinted lens of the group, not as it really is.

Group think is very unhealthy. It's what leads to war, racism and class warfare. Every one of us is an *individual* and unique in all the world.

The Police

When I was growing up, a child of the fifties, I was always taught, "The policeman is your friend." And that might have been true back then. But today while a policeman might be your friend, the *police* are *not*.

I grew up in Pennsylvania and Pennsylvania is unique in that most of the state's municipalities are boroughs and townships. Hundreds of them. Many of them have populations of three or four, maybe ten thousand people. And back then each borough or township had its own part-time mayor and town council, its own volunteer fire department and usually just one police car. This made policing interesting and effective. Crime was very low.

Basically, it was community policing. The policeman knew many of the residents by name. He knew who the good boys were and who the bad boys were. He knew if there was a light on that shouldn't have been late at night in Espy's Drug Store, if there was a strange car behind Bishoff's Deli or odd goings on at the Meyer's house while they were on vacation. He knew the community and his job was to make sure everything was copacetic.

If young Eddie rolled through a stop sign, as likely as not the policeman would have stopped him and the conversation would have gone something like this:

"Now, Eddie, you know what stop means. I've seen you run this sign before. And if I catch you doing it again I'm going to have to write you a ticket. You don't want that, do you?"

"No sir, Sergeant Schultz. I'll be more careful."

Sergeant Shultz knew Eddie was a good kid and he really *didn't* want to give him a ticket. He just wanted the intersection to be safe. And Eddie probably always stopped at that intersection after his little chat with the police.

Most boroughs and townships had three policemen, each working an eight-hour shift. And in those days the police walked a lot. Up one street and down the next. Sometimes helping an old lady take her groceries into the house. Other times checking the lock on the barbershop door. The police were an integral part of the community.

How times have changed. Today the police cover pretty big territory. And they do it all in cars loaded with computers and a lot of high power weaponry. About the only time you see a policeman out of his car is when he's giving someone a two hundred dollar ticket for doing seventy in a sixty zone or on his way into a convenience store to buy more donuts. In most cases he's a stranger in the territory he's policing. This isn't an indictment of the individual police officer, rather of the whole system.

Even in large cities, policing could and should be a neighborhood endeavor. A little interaction and mutual respect would go a long way toward keeping the neighborhood safe.

Today the policeman is mostly a tax collector. He cruises around in his car looking for people going just a little too fast, making an improper turn or driving with expired paperwork. The kinds of things that generate revenue.

The police prevent very little crime. The most they can do is show up sometime after the fact and try to figure out who might have done it, but the lion's share of crimes go unsolved.

And today the police just aren't very nice. Recently while driving home I was stopped by police with a roadblock. They were stopping every car. I was very nice and had a big fake smile on my face. The cop was *most unpleasant*. The conversation went like this:

"Yes sir. What can I do for you?

"Safety check."

"Was I doing something unsafe?"

"Drivers license, registration and insurance card."

"I hope I wasn't doing anything unsafe."

"Drivers license, registration and insurance card."

He took the papers, scrutinized them, then walked around to the back of the car and compared the registration card to the license plate number. Then he swaggered back to my window and said, "You can go now."

"Thank you. Am I safe now?"

"You can go now."

The police feel no need to converse with you, explain what they're doing or even be civil anymore. They all seem to have an attitude problem. And why are people being stopped en mass these days for paper checks, seat belt checks or sobriety checks? Is it like being at the airport? Are we all guilty now until we prove our innocence? And while the police are busy checking everybody's paperwork the gas station is being robbed.

But what's most disturbing to me about the police is that they've been federalized. And one hallmark of a police state is a national police force. Lots and lots of Homeland Security and stimulus money went to police departments all over the country. Money that was used to buy all those nifty non-lethal tasers that scores of people die from every year, bigger and badder guns, riot gear, spy cameras and armored vehicles -- urban tanks. Are they getting ready for something they haven't told us about?

And police violence and brutality is on the increase. Hardly a day goes by when we don't read about some atrocity in which an innocent person was terrorized, injured or killed by the police.

And one thing the police *really* don't like is someone photographing their abuse of someone. Recently the police were roughing up someone's next door neighbor. He went outside on his front lawn and started video taping. He was arrested for using a video camera on his own property. Further, he was told if he resisted they'd also confiscate his camera.

This one was all over the Internet a while back. An engineering student in college whose primary interest was rail transportation, used his summer break to travel throughout the northeast and photograph trains. No problem until he got to Baltimore. There he got hassled to no end. The police -- several of them -- were all over this kid. Apparently in Baltimore it's against the law to take a picture of a train. It's not but the police often just make up the law. To his credit the kid held his ground. He was very polite but insisted they cite the law that says it's illegal to photograph a train. They said, "Haven't you heard about 911? Everything's different now." It sure is but that doesn't mean you can't take a picture of a train.

Two more. These happened within a couple of days of each other.

In the first situation the police -- a dozen of them with assault weapons ready and aimed -- broke down a man's door in California, terrorizing him and his children. The man and his children were taken to a police car where they were forced to stay for more than two hours in the hot sun with no air conditioning while the police rifled through the house looking for who knows what. Finally the man and his children were released from custody when it was determined the person they were looking for wasn't there. They were looking for the man's ex-wife.

And it wasn't just the local police who were looking for her. The feds were along on the raid, as well. The SWAT team was federal. Her "crime"? Delinquent student loan payments. And yes, the Department of Education has its own SWAT team. And apparently this is their new way to collect a debt.

A couple of days later in Pennsylvania the same thing happened. This time terrorizing a man, his wife and small children. The cops aimed their guns with laser sights at the children and the family pet. This time they were looking for a woman who hadn't lived in the house for more than two years and whom the current renters had never even met. This occurred in Allegheny County, Pennsylvania where renters have to register their address. The cops were too lazy or too inept to check the county records before conducting their violent raid on an innocent family.

Here's another one -- *as I write*. This kind of stuff is happening *every day*. A man suspected of a relatively minor crime. He's on the street lying face down. He put up no resistance. The police (six of them) tased him -- *five times* -- after which he was still breathing. So they beat him to death. There's video of the whole thing. The man's neighbors described him as a kind, gentle man who wouldn't have hurt a fly. Well, he won't be hurting any flies now, will he?

Whenever there's a police investigation following a citizen complaint, the conclusion is that the police were within their rights and following procedure. If so, this makes current procedure a pretty scary thing.

And new federal wiretapping (!) laws make it a crime to photograph or video tape the police when they're up to no good. If convicted you could get up to fifteen years in prison.

The more the federal government gets involved with the police, the more the police start to look like the military, and that's not a good thing.

Small Business

When's the last time you saw a locally owned super market, pet store, department store, car dealership, drug store, hardware store, medical practice -- or almost anything else?

Since our earliest days, small business has been the backbone of our economy. Owning a business lifted a lot of people into the middle class and small businesses created most of the jobs.

Remember what fascism is: a country run by the government, big corporations and banks. And if you're a big corporation the easiest way to dominate or monopolize your market segment is to have the government legislate all the small guys out of business. Taxes and regulations are so burdensome for small businesses that many of them can't survive because only the big players can afford to stay in the game.

Years ago if you had a rich uncle who could lend you a little money, you could hang up a sign and go into business. And with some time and hard work you might even prosper. Today, assuming you could even get one, it would take a hefty bank loan just to deal with the permits, taxes, fees, inspections and regulations *before* you open your doors.

Thanks to government taxes and regulations this is no longer a country where someone with a good idea, a goal and some hard work can make it. Sure, a few people do, but they're very much in the minority.

So as more and more small businesses bite the dust, their former owners have to enter the workforce as employees -- often for the same big corporations that put them out of business.

Everything's big now. Big stores. Big banks. Big government. And none of them care diddly squat about you; you're just an account number. All they want is your money.

If this country is ever to recover from our current economic mess it will be entrepreneurs with good ideas who get the job done. The innovators. We need to get the government as far away from small business as possible.

The Department of Energy

Why we put the government in charge of anything we want more of, I don't know. If the government were in charge of the Sahara Desert, in six months there would be a sand shortage.

This country is loaded with natural resources. We have lots of coal. And Texas, the Gulf coast and Alaska are dripping with oil, while Pennsylvania has enough natural gas to power the entire universe for a zillion years.

All these fossil fuels and we import much of our oil, and often from countries we've pissed off so badly that it's a wonder they're willing to sell us anything.

We don't drill because the government and its buddies in the environmental movement have made it almost impossible. You can't drill a new well until you can prove you won't deface four acres of beautiful tundra or kill eleven fish.

We all want to drive our cars and heat and cool our homes, but we don't want to pay the price for modern civilization, which means we might have to smudge a miniscule portion of the earth to get what we need. The government doesn't want any fish to die while we extract oil, but it's just fine that a lot of birds get mutilated by windmills.

For years the Alaska pipeline was held up by the government and the environmentalists who ranted hysterically about how it would destroy the tundra and ruin the habitat of the caribou. The tundra is barren land where very little grows, so I don't know what they thought we were going to destroy, and as it turned out, the caribou actually liked the pipeline. It helped keep them warm in winter.

But how much damage *could* the pipeline have done to Alaska? Think of it this way. Take an acre of ground. Then run a thin thread down the middle of it. That's the pipeline. I think the question is self-answering.

The government is constantly telling us we need to find alternative sources of energy and reduce our dependence on fossil fuels. And it keeps throwing your tax dollars at technologies that don't work unless they're subsidized -- even more tax dollars.

Things like ethanol, discussed earlier. Besides the ridiculous subsidies and the related rise in food prices, it takes more energy to produce ethanol than it provides. In fact, it takes a lot of oil to produce ethanol. What kind if insane technology is that?

Several years ago there *was* an interesting new technology: home fuel cells. As usual, this new technology didn't come from the government or corporate behemoths. It came from independent scientists, entrepreneurs and back yard tinkerers. They had the fuel cell technology to the point where for four or five thousand dollars you could buy a fuel cell and power your entire house for about two hundred bucks a year. And no pollution.

The fuel cells were about six months from being on the market and a number of companies were putting people on the waiting list for one of the first ones. I was on one of the waiting lists.

There was one very big problem with the fuel cells. If you bought one, you were *off the grid*. That would be competition for Con Ed, Duke Energy and all those other big energy companies with last century's technology. But they *are* the big guys, and before the fuel cells could hit the market, the patents were all bought up for sizable sums of money and put on a shelf somewhere to gather dust.

People have come up with all kinds of alternative ways to provide energy. Magnets, water and all kinds of things. Several inventors have developed cars that run on water. Water is made up of hydrogen and oxygen. The oxygen is separated from the hydrogen which powers the car. The exhaust is oxygen. Every time someone gets close to bringing his engine to market, it suddenly disappears. Or *he* does. Poof. Now you see, now you don't.

Can't have that. The oil companies are very powerful and they're not about to allow any serious competition.

The government doesn't want you to have energy independence. It doesn't want you to have *any* kind of independence. The government lies. All governments lie. What the government wants is your tax money to subsidize its corporate friends. And its corporate friends want to provide you with less energy at higher prices.

Welfare

One of the most important and insidious ways the government maintains and increases its power over the citizens is by creating dependency. People dependent on the government for basic necessities will seldom rock the boat.

Hence, the welfare system. There are welfare programs on top of welfare programs on top of welfare programs. And even overlapping welfare programs. The government will help you pay your rent, pay your cell phone bill, assist you with car repairs and feed your children breakfast. The list of personal activities the government involves itself in is nearly endless.

There are problems with this. First of all, they're all unconstitutional. Nothing in the constitution gives the government the power or the right to be involved in any of these endeavors. Secondly, once one becomes dependent on the government to subsidize his lifestyle, he'll seldom do anything to end the subsidy. Indeed, we have multi generations of families on welfare. It becomes a way of life.

Beyond that, the government's welfare programs are costly beyond imagination, administering very little welfare for the money collected in taxes from those paying the bills.

Any reasonable and intelligent person has to realize that when a bloated bureaucracy in Washington is feeding children breakfast or lunch in school, the administrative overhead has to be enormous. And it is.

How does the cost of welfare provided by the government compare with that provided by charities? According to the last figures I have on the cost of welfare from Washington, the government has to take in $4.20 to administer $1.00 in actual welfare. This figure is a few years old, so it's probably even worse now. How does that compare to private charitable efforts? The Salvation Army, for example only needs to take in about $1.10 to give $1.00 in assistance.

Why? Because the Salvation Army and many more organizations like it depend on volunteers; people donating their time for the cause. And there's no bureaucracy.

Whether it's the Salvation Army, Goodwill, Habitat for Humanity, Meals on Wheels, community organizations, churches, synagogues and mosques or any of the plethora of other private organizations dedicated to helping people in need, the job is always done more cost effectively, more meaningfully and personally than anything doled out by the government.

And unlike the government, which *encourages dependency*, most private charities encourage and assist people to get back on their feet and become self-supporting again.

And like all other government programs, the welfare system keeps growing and growing and growing. We now have nearly fifty million people receiving food stamps. Personally, I find it hard to believe that there are fifty million Americans who can't afford to go grocery shopping.

And like most government programs, the real beneficiaries of the Food Stamp program aren't the poor; they're some of those rich folks with clout and bags full of money to spread around the whorehouse. It was the *corporate farming industry* that lobbied congress to enact the Food Stamp legislation, so they could sell more food. In particular, they wanted to sell more packaged goods, such as frozen dinners and snack foods, the kinds of products people with Food Stamps are likely to purchase with their found money. Whenever the government announces a program to help the little guy, some rich guy's getting even richer.

When bureaucrats in Washington are paying personal phone bills (Who do you think lobbied for that one?), feeding your children lunch, fixing cars and paying rent, you *know* things are out of control. And it just keeps growing. As I write this, the government is planning on becoming the biggest landlord in the country, with plans to ultimately own about a million residential rental houses.

There's no end to the nonsense the government will involve itself in if we let it. The problem is that we do. Taking care of the poor, the sick, the disabled and others less fortunate than most, has always been something done very well by private charitable organizations. Indeed, before the government got its claws into welfare, people weren't dropping dead in the streets from starvation. The sick weren't turned away by doctors. And children ate lunch.

The federal welfare system is one more gigantic government boondoggle we need to put an end to. We need to discourage dependency and encourage self reliance. And in the process, we'll save hundreds of billions of dollars, three fourths of which just feed the bureaucracy.

Highways and Public Transportation

Why is the government in charge of all public transportation? Like nearly everything else, couldn't the free market do this? It can and used to. Until forty or fifty years ago nearly all public transit was provided by private companies. Where I grew up there were thirty privately operated transit companies.

I had choices. I had four ways to get downtown with each provider competing for my fare. I could take the train, an express bus, a local bus or a trolley.

At the time they were forcibly taken over by the government twenty-eight of the thirty companies were earning a profit and paying taxes. Now the government runs the transit system and the train is gone, as is the express bus and trolley. The service stinks and the system is millions of dollars in the red every year. This means that people who don't use public transit have to subsidize those who do.

In the city in which I most recently lived, you can't start your own transit company; it's a government monopoly. And every time someone gets on a city bus or light rail train, the *subsidy* is four dollars. That's right, the government *loses* four dollars per rider. But once the government gets its claws into something, no matter how badly it fails, it never gives up its power.

And now the subsidies even come from Washington. This means someone in a small town in West Virginia has to pay for someone to ride a bus in Seattle.

A few years ago I lived in an apartment complex a *block away from a shopping mall*. The city-owned transit system had just acquired a fleet of small thirty passenger buses and had to do *something* with them. One of those things was establishing a route between the apartment complex and the mall -- one block away. Every twenty minutes, all day long, the bus would make its loop from the apartment complex to the mall and back. Only once did I ever see anyone on the bus.

But the transit system got a grant from the federal government and had to spend it on *something*. It didn't really matter what, but it never does. It doesn't matter to them. It's *your* money, not theirs.

Road building makes about as much sense as public transportation. Every year, billions are wasted on ridiculous road building projects. The federal government doles out a lot of highway construction money, and with that money comes an entire ball of strings.

Remember that the government has no money of its own. Every dime it spends, is taken from you in taxes. It takes your money, skims its sizable part off the top, then sends the rest back to you but tells you how to spend it.

In many cases if a state wants to widen a portion of an Interstate highway, the new lane must be designated as an HOV lane. High occupancy vehicle. What we have now is the government taxing behavior. You pay for the HOV lane but you're not allowed to drive on it unless you have a passenger. That's right, one passenger. Since when is two people in a car high occupancy?

The official explanation for this nonsense is that the government is trying to encourage carpooling. I can just hear that conversation:

"Hey Fred, if you're willing to leave for work a half hour earlier you can ride with me and we can drive in the left lane!"

"The left lane! Cool. Let's do it."

So anyway, you're cruising down the Interstate, alone in your car. You're in the center lane passing a slow-moving old couple poking along in the HOV lane. Why isn't the left lane a high-speed lane or an express lane? Anything that might keep traffic moving better? Because it's government's job to tell you what to do, not make your life easier.

Another local project. This city had a six lane street with very high congestion in the morning and afternoon rush hours. The city came forth with a plan -- with much of the money and strings coming from Washington. The street was going to be widened to eight lanes and turned into an expressway.

And indeed it was. What we weren't told was that the two new lanes were for buses only. Millions and millions of dollars spent so the city buses could cruise down the road in their own special lanes. And they do. Every twenty minutes or so, a city bus rolls down one of its special lanes with four passengers on board.

Whether it's public transit or road building, funding always comes with strings. And the strings are connected to the puppet masters. There's no reason states and municipalities can't build their own roads, and do so more economically and sensibly.

In fact there's a case to be made for *privately* built roads. Many large real estate developers build their own roads. Miles of them. Or a privately built toll road. Toll roads are fair because the only people who pay for them are the ones who actually use them.

And why can't someone start his own bus company or passenger train system? We can't have a privately owned passenger train system because the federal government took that over, too. Amtrak. The service is terrible, most routes cost more than flying, the trains are almost always late and every year or so one of the trains mysteriously leaps of the tracks and kills a bunch of people.

One more way to reduce spending by billions of dollars and balance the budget: Get the government out of the transportation business, which it has no constitutional right to be in.

Victimless Crime

Isn't the term *victimless* crime an oxymoron? If there's no victim, how can there be a crime? Victimless crimes are nothing more than the state deciding how you should act, even if you're not causing harm to anyone else. Basically, victimless crimes are crimes against the state. The government makes up some stupid rule and you have to obey it.

Victimless crimes include recreational drug use, gambling, prostitution, operating a motorcycle without a helmet and almost anything that's fun if you're under age.

We've already covered drugs, so I won't spend much time on this one, other than to remind you that while some illegal drugs can be harmful, so can the drugs your doctor gives you. Legal drugs aren't necessarily safe and illegal drugs aren't necessarily dangerous. Being illegal doesn't in and of itself make a drug bad, it just makes it illegal. If marijuana weren't so easy to grow and could be synthesized and sold in pill form with a doctor's prescription for thirty bucks a pop, it would be legal *tomorrow*.

Gambling is an interesting one, because it shows just how duplicitous the government really is.

Years ago the mob ran most of the gambling operations. The popular game was called "the numbers". It was an honest game because you picked your number for the day and the winning number was the closing number of the stock market. They usually used the Dow Jones. There was a winning number every day.

Because playing the numbers was as illegal as smoking marijuana, you had to bet on your number pretty much like you have to buy pot today. Today you have drug dealers and back then you had numbers runners.

The government propaganda against the numbers game was relentless. It was unfair to the poor. The odds of winning were low. The profits financed all kinds of nefarious activities. Yadda, yadda, yeah, yeah.

The truth of the matter is the government was against the numbers because it saw this type of gambling as very profitable and it wanted in on the action. But the government hates competition because whenever it has to compete honestly with anything else, it loses. So first the government had to put the numbers out of business, which it did.

Suddenly gambling was *good*. Because it was *for the children*. The Education Lottery. Gambling is good if it's *for the children*. The so-called education lotteries have taken in a blue zillion dollars over the years, but the schools still constantly whine about not having enough money. And they certainly haven't gotten any better.

But all the reasons the numbers game was bad also apply to the governments' lotteries. It's typically the poor who play. The odds of winning are actually *lower* in the government lottery than they were with the numbers game. And the profits from the lotteries still finance a lot of nefarious activities. Government activities. Given my choice I'd rather finance the mob. At least it provided a few useful things and didn't force me to buy them.

Prostitution. There's a *reason* it's called the world's oldest profession. Because it is. Throughout history there have always been some guys who just can't get girls on their own merits. And because it's instinctive for the male of every species to want to spread that seed around -- even if only recreationally -- men who can't get women on their looks, their money, their intelligence, their sense of humor, their charm or even their line of bullshit, some are going to pay to play.

And because it's one big marketplace out there, some women are going to see this need as a way to make a living. Still possessing some portion of the afore-mentioned qualities, I've never patronized a prostitute. Besides, I've always preferred a healthy dose of love along with my sex. But it's not my place to judge some other guy's circumstances, nor those of a woman willing to do business with him.

Regardless of the fact that I believe it has to be a rather unpleasant way to make a living, I don't believe it should be illegal. If there's one thing you own that the government should never be able to take away or regulate, it's your own body. and if you want to rent it to someone for half an hour, it's strictly your business.

The idea that the police should be rounding people up and throwing them in jail for having sex is ludicrous. Even if there was money involved. If a guy takes a woman out for an expensive dinner, complete with fine wine and one of those chocolate mega-calorie desserts, then takes her home and has sex with her, there was money involved, too. It just wasn't a formal business arrangement. More of an understanding. Wink, nod.

If you're under age, almost anything fun is illegal. I have to admit that I don't have all the answers on this one, but what I do know is that the government's arbitrary age requirements aren't one of them.

In most states, driving a car if you're under sixteen is illegal. Who decided that magically, at the age of sixteen every kid has the good sense and maturity to operate a motor vehicle? I've known fourteen year-olds who should have been allowed to drive. I've also known fifty year-olds who never should have been given a license. But the government decrees that at sixteen any kid should be allowed to get behind the wheel of two tons of steel and cruise down the highway.

Who should decide, and how? My first thought was that since parents know their children better than anyone else, maybe the decision should be theirs. But these days, it seems a lot of parents need parents of their own.

If not the government, who? Here's an idea. How about insurance companies? More than anyone else, they have a financial stake in the matter. They won't want to insure anyone they feel isn't ready to drive a car. They could provide the driver training and the road test as a prerequisite to being insured and allowed to drive. Perhaps some people could drive at fourteen or fifteen, while others would never be allowed on the road.

You can drive a car at sixteen but you can't purchase tobacco until you're eighteen. And you can't drink alcohol until you're twenty-one. You can put on a uniform, put a high-power rifle in your hand, go off to some foreign country and murder a stranger, but you can't have a beer afterward.

In fact, after you come home from shooting strangers in some foreign country, you can get married, buy a car, get yourself some credit cards and buy a house. You can even become a parent. That's a lot of adult responsibility. But you still can't buy a beer. Does any of this make any sense. I mean *really*?

In many countries parents allow their children to drink. Not six year-olds, but older children. They teach their children moderation and let them acquire a taste for grownup beverages slowly and responsibly. I allowed my step-daughter to drink, *at home*, one, *maybe* two, when she was in her teens. I have a friend with two children. Her sixteen year-old son gets to sit at the table with the grownups and have *one* beer. Her twelve year-old daughter gets to choose between orange juice and iced tea.

The point is, everything the government does is arbitrary and seldom makes any sense. Crime is something harmful you do to someone else, not what you do to yourself. You have a right to treat yourself well or treat yourself poorly. And if you're a responsible person you should have the right to do things at the age at which you are ready and able, not when some arbitrary government edict tells you you're allowed to.

In a normal, sane world with a government under control, there would be no such thing as a *victimless* crime.

---

* * *

I could write another hundred pages on government ineptitude and absurdity, BUT-I-THINK-YOU-GET-THE-POINT.

These and *countless other government schemes* have cost you your freedom and a lot of money. *Trillions and trillions* of wasted dollars that could and should have remained in your pocket. And in case you weren't sure, here's what *one* trillion dollars looks like.

$1,000,000,000,000.00

How Did All This Happen?

Herein, I'm going to use the term "you". By "you" I mean the majority of Americans. Then again, I *might* mean *you*.

Hey.

Everything previously discussed -- all the government boondoggles, failed programs, corruption, theft, fraud and abuses -- have occurred because there was no opposition to them.

Every time there's a new attempt to take more freedom with yet another new federal agency or program, more taxes, or the drumbeats for a new undeclared war, people say, "Americans will never stand for that." My response is always, "Yes they will. They *always* do." Because they always do.

We complain a little bit, then we just accept it. No matter how stupid, expensive or intrusive it is. The government tells us how much water our toilet can flush, what kind of light bulbs we're allowed to use, who we're allowed to hire and for how much money whether or not we're allowed to drill for our own oil, and a blue zillion other things it has no business involving itself in. And our response is *always* the same:

"Duh, okay."

Apparently you *like* having your freedom taken from you, your earnings and savings stolen from you and people all over the world killed in your name. Because you do *nothing* to stop it.

No matter how many times politicians lie to you, or how dishonest or corrupt they are, you just keep sending them back to engage in more mischief. Amazingly, *a politician's reward for doing bad things is to be reelected.*

In every election campaign, politicians rich with "donations" from their *real* constituents tell you anything you want to hear and you give them your vote. And deep in your heart of hearts, you *know* they're lying to you, but you vote for them, anyway. If what they were saying last week wasn't working, they simply change their position and say something new. Whatever you want to hear. Whatever you'll believe.

In a country of three hundred million people, is it not possible to find five hundred or so honest ones? Apparently not.

Way back in the introduction to his book, I wrote that if you don't know where you were, you can't understand where you are or where you're headed. If a politician has repeatedly lied to you in the past, he's gonna lie to you again in the future. If every government program has cost more than it said it would or failed to meet its stated goals, the same thing will happen next time. The future is a screen on which we project the past.

But we never seem to learn our lessons. Albert Einstein defined insanity as doing the same thing over and over and each time expecting a different result.

We must be insane.

Wake up! If a politician is promoted by CNN, Fox News, the Wall Street Journal or the big banks and corporations, he's your enemy. The only honest politician is the one the big inside players are afraid of. Just as you should fear the government that fears its citizens, the ruling elite fear the politician who tells the truth.

Or do we just not care any more? I'm reminded of the old Flip Wilson joke:

"Good afternoon, sir. I'm taking a confidential survey. Do you think Americans are ignorant and apathetic?"

"I don't know and I don't care."

Is that how far we've sunk? Has our inner being been hollowed out to the point where as long as we have our cable TV, late model car and a wallet full of credit cards, we just don't care what happens?

Judging from your response (or non response) to anything and everything the government does, that would appear to be the case. And yet, I still believe that if enough people awaken from their sleep state and finally rise up, we might still have a chance to avoid a train wreck with national bankruptcy and tyranny.

But it will take a lot of people and we have precious little time left. Are you going to wake up or continue to sleepwalk your way into financial, political and social ruin?

It's time to stand up and be a *real* American, while you still can.

Over the years, a number of my friends have been immigrants. People who courageously left everything they knew and came here to make a better life for themselves. I have several friends from the former Soviet Union, and they all have the same thing to say about Americans. Almost verbatim:

"Americans are the dumbest people on the planet. All our lives we hoped to be free. Americans had their freedom handed to them and they're just throwing it away."

Maybe we *are* the dumbest people on the planet.

Sometimes the torch of freedom is dwindled down to just a match, but it's never snuffed out entirely. In writing this book, I'm hoping to add a little oxygen to the match.

The clock is ticking and we're nearing the midnight hour. The fat lady ain't sung yet. But she's waiting in the wings.

If things are going to turn around, *you're* going to have to be part of it. You and everybody you know. Will you stand to defend your freedom?

For once?

Finally?

Why Do All Government Programs Fail?

We can't seem to win a war, including the war on poverty and the war on drugs, our children don't learn, Social Security is bankrupt, public transit is a money pit and crime is high, yet the government takes in and spends *trillions* of dollars a year -- and borrows a trillion or two more.

Why does nothing seem to work?

First of all, some things don't have "solutions". You can't stop some people from making decisions that lead them into or keep them in poverty. And you can't make people stop putting things they like in their mouth. So a lot of what government tries to change or correct can't really be fixed by anybody.

But the important thing to understand is that government programs are *designed* to fail. Remember way back in the beginning of this book when I told you government isn't here for you; it's here for itself. Government is organized monopoly force. As soon as government goes beyond its very few legitimate functions it becomes a criminal enterprise. It takes money by force and spends it as it chooses.

It never gives up a program without a serious fight and it never shrinks itself voluntarily. Government is like a cancer. It just keeps growing and growing, taking and taking.

Like all organisms, even social ones, government has a self-preservation instinct and it never ceases in its lust for power.

Government wants its programs to fail? Let's create a little analogy. Let's say you own a business and within that business are three different divisions. Two of them are successful and profitable, but one has been failing for some time.

What do you do with the two divisions that are profitable? You might expand them, add to your product line, maybe hire more employees, right? If in spite of repeated efforts, the third division always loses money, you'd probably shut it down or sell it off to someone who thinks he might be able to do a better job.

That's how the market works. You expand what works and you shrink or eliminate what doesn't. Because in the real marketplace if you don't provide a good product or service, you go out of business. You have competition and to prosper you have to be better -- or at least as good.

Government is the exact opposite. If government *succeeds* it goes out of business. Critical thinking time again. Let's take the war on poverty which dates back to the 1960s. Yes, we've been at war with poverty for a half century and have as much poverty as we've ever had.

But what if -- *what if* -- by some miracle there were no more poor people left by, say, 1980? We actually won the war on poverty. Suddenly there would no longer be any need for the thousands of federal troops fighting all that poverty. No need for all those government buildings that house the thousands of poverty-fighting warriors. No need to collect all that tax money. The anti-poverty program would be *out of business*.

So the best thing the government can do is keep *trying* to fight poverty. And when it fails, which it always does, unlike the failing division in your company, it actually *grows* and gets *more* money. "We're making progress in the war on poverty. We just need more money and more caseworkers." The more it fails, the more power and the more money it gets.

Why do the schools fail? Because the more they fail, the more money they get. When they fail it's because they don't have enough teachers, the teachers aren't paid enough, they don't have nice new buildings, there are too many students in the classroom. The excuses are endless and the solution is always more people and more money.

I went to school in a building built in 1893. We never

had air conditioning and we had heat sometimes. The teachers weren't paid very much, there were no teaching assistants and the average class size was thirty-five. And you know what? We learned. More than that, there was only one unwanted pregnancy, no drugs, no assaults on students or teachers, no weapons or metal detectors. But that was then.

The point is if we learned in those conditions, all the things they're whining about today can't be the cause the horrible state of government schools. No, it's all about growing the system and taking in more tax money. The school system has become a top heavy bureaucracy with entirely too many over-paid administrators.

Have you ever wondered why any time you have to deal with the government, it seems to take forever and require endless forms to be filled out, many times redundantly? Because government has to keep its enormous workforce busy doing something. It doesn't have to be anything useful, just *something*.

Why haven't we either won the wars in Afghanistan and Iraq or come home? Because the government loves a good L-O-N-G war. The military (part of the government) grows, the defense contractors get really, really rich and the banks make out like bandits. It's been said that war is the health of the state and the wealth of the banks. Because governments typically don't finance wars with taxes; they finance them by borrowing. Of course, later on, *we* have to pay back the loans through taxes after the fact.

And it's not just the military that grows. Countless civilian government agencies grow to support the military's activities. And this time, in addition to the wars on the Afghans and Iraqis, here at home the CIA, NSA, Homeland Security, FEMA, TSA and who knows how many other government agencies are waging war on the American people. Oh, I'm sorry. I meant keeping us safe.

Just as with the war in Vietnam, which seemed to last

forever (and we lost), our current wars are going to drag on as long as the people will allow them to. And just as with the Vietnam war, the defense contractors are uncorking the Champaign, the bankers are counting their money and the government is doing what it does best -- growing.

Here's an interesting what if? What if the eighty or ninety people who actually belong to al Qaeda decided they were wrong They didn't really hate us. They apologized for their past behavior and promised to be our friends forever? And they did. They came over here and did volunteer work and became model citizens.

There would be a big and immediate government problem. What to do with its enormous multi-billion dollar Homeland Security bureaucracy? Can't shut it down. Government *never* does that. You can bet there will be another terrorist attack, real or home grown. And then they'll demand more money, more personnel and more unpleasant rules. It's just the way it works. The Soviet Union finally collapsed because the bureaucracy was so huge and bloated that the whole system just caved in on itself.

So unlike life out here in the real world, any time the government might actually succeed at something or meet its goals, whatever department was responsible for it would have to go out of business.

It's the same on the local level. The police, for example. If crime goes up they get more money. And they always need more money. Money for more new police cars, more radar, more serious weaponry, more surveillance equipment, more employees. Always more. They never quite seem to get a handle on crime. But if they just had more money.

Government is a very strange animal. Nothing it does would allow it to survive in the real world. Going back to the business analogy, what if you did what the government does with the division of your company that was losing money? What if you kept throwing more and more money at it and kept hiring more and more employees? How long would you stay in business? Ahh...but what if you could force people to give you all the money you wanted for that losing division of your company? You could keep doing a lousy job forever, couldn't you?

Massive theft and Fraud

Once a government goes past its legitimate functions of protecting the citizens from aggression, protecting their rights, maintaining fair and free trade and coining honest money, just about everything else it does involves activities, as mentioned earlier in this book, which would put you or me in prison.

Once outside its only proper roles, government activities always consist of stealing, fraud or force. The current economic crisis is the predictable result of decades of all three.

Ever since Roosevelt's New Deal, we've had a program called Social Security. This was sold to us as a retirement investment program to ensure a livable income in our later years. The money was put into a "trust fund" and we each had an account where our funds were securely held.

Here's the force part: It wasn't voluntary. *Everybody* was forced into the program, regardless of his ability to pay, personal wealth or desire to plan differently.

Now here's the fraud part: There was never any trust fund and no one had a personal account. Consequently, no money was invested, meaning money paid in didn't earn interest or otherwise increase in value.

And here's the stealing part: The money's all gone. The system is broke. In other words, the government stole and spent your retirement money and replaced it with IOUs. And what are the IOUs? They're money the government is planning to steal from your children, or even those not born yet, to replace the money the government fraudulently converted for its own uses from your "trust fund".

Beyond all that, the government keeps changing the rules as time goes on. Social Security "benefits" are increased, decreased or have all sorts of new rules attached to them to cater to political demands or to juggle the books. Few people end up getting back the all money they put into Social Security over their working life, let alone see a positive return on their investment.

If the government were honest and actually *did* invest your money, just putting it in a bank account at four or five percent interest, you'd be able to retire in style. As Albert Einstein said, "The most powerful force in the universe is compound interest."

Indeed, if you were able to put the same amount of money into a whole life insurance policy, that you paid into Social Security, you'd have a ton of money by the time you retired. And there would be no rules or strings attached. You'd just have it to do with as you pleased. And if you died before you spent it all, you could leave the rest to your children.

The government is constantly reassuring us that the "trust fund" is solvent until twenty something or other. But in fact, it's not. It's broke. Translating from Governmentese to English, what that means is the government thinks it can collect enough in taxes from other people to keep sending out checks until sometime in the not too distant future, at which time they don't have a clue as to where the money will come from.

Because it spent it. *Your retirement money*. That's theft. If you or I did that, we'd be living in a place with guards and high walls. When the government steals, no one goes to jail, they just get reelected.

And as I've said repeatedly through this book, the government always takes care of its own. Your congressman doesn't pay into Social Security; he's exempt. The government has its own very good retirement program where the funds really are invested. No, they're not stupid. They're counting on your being stupid.

So where did your Social Security money go? Or for that matter, all the rest of your tax money? The truth is that nobody really knows for sure. Some of it can be traced and accounted for, but billions, actually trillions of dollars have just disappeared. Every year, hundreds of billions of dollars are allocated for secret or classified activities. Things even congress isn't allowed to know about. How much accountability do you think is attached to that money? Just give us the money and don't ask questions.

In Afghanistan and Iraq, pallets piled high with one hundred dollar bills were delivered and just spread around. No one knows for sure where it went, but it's gone. In congressional testimony, the Pentagon admitted it was *unable to account for more than a trillion dollars*. How do you lose track of a trillion dollars?

The bailouts which were part of the "stimulus packages" were just more theft. Was it your fault the Fed created massive amounts of money for banks to lend? Was it your fault banks made ridiculous loans exceeding the value of houses being financed, and to people they knew couldn't repay? Was it your fault the big Wall Street investment houses fraudulently packaged those loans and sold them to unwitting investors? Was it your fault Fannie Mae and Freddie Mac, which were only supposed to guarantee good loans, lowered their standards to accepting anything with paper and ink?

Why did they do this? Were they stupid? No, they were smart. They made billions of dollars, and they knew when all the bad stuff hit the fan, *you'd* be stuck with the bill.

More theft on a grand scale.

If the people who've been systematically stealing from us for the past several decades were tried and convicted, there wouldn't be enough prisons to hold them all. They're criminals.

And now that the Fed has all but destroyed the once mighty dollar, it's time to bend over and get screwed again. This time it's new taxes. I'm sorry. I meant revenue enhancements and closing loopholes. And of course, a new round of inflation, this time on steroids. And remember, inflation is just another form of taxation. Why? Because every time the government steals and gets caught with its pants down (which shouldn't be confused with your congressman getting caught with his pants down), or otherwise makes a big mess of something -- *we* have to sacrifice.

Why do *we* have to sacrifice? *We* didn't make the mess. They make a big mess and we sacrifice. See how it works?

I've known a lot of very wealthy people in my life. I've eaten in fancy restaurants with them (if they paid), I've been on their fancy boats and flown on their nifty planes. And I've attended some of their lavish parties. Most of the rich people I've known got that way by being smart and working hard. I've always admired them and never envied them. And I've never thought I was entitled to any of their money just because they had more than they needed.

The government is another story. Wealthy people are just one more source of revenue. More theft. Why is the government entitled to it just because they have it?

And no matter how much money the government steals from those of us out here in the real world, it just can't seem to balance its books or figure out where it all goes. Why not? *It's not their money.*

To get a better idea of how the government views your money, let's imagine someone gave you a hundred dollars and told you to use it to buy something nice for yourself. You'd go to the mall and shop carefully for something you'd really like to have, wouldn't you?

Now suppose the same person gave you a hundred dollars and told you to spend it on a friend. You'd want to buy something nice for your friend, but you wouldn't be quite as careful or selective as you would have been if you were spending it on yourself.

In the third scenario, the same person gives you a

hundred dollars and instructs you to buy something for a total stranger. How much effort would you put into *that* mission?

The third example is the government. It takes money from someone and spends it on a stranger. But it's worse than that. Given your instructions to buy something for a stranger, even though you wouldn't have shopped very hard, you probably would have spent the money -- because you're honest. When the government is at the mall, it checks to make sure no one is looking, then puts fifty in its pocket and spends the other fifty on the stranger.

Governments steal. They all do. Because they can. And our government will keep stealing from us as long as we allow it to.

What's really interesting to me is the odds. There are three hundred million people living in this country. And 546 thieves. One would think three hundred million people could defeat 546 bad guys. The 546 bad guys consist of the Senate, the House, the President and Vice-President and nine guys in black robes. They're the ones who write the tax laws, give your money to the bureaucracy and empower it to do all its dastardly deeds.

They're the criminals. They're the ones who engage in massive theft -- trillions and trillions and trillions of dollars taken from people who actually work for a living -- pass it around to their rich and powerful friends and squander the rest. And when they make a really big mess, they just take some more. Because our job is to sacrifice.

And we just keep sending them back to do it again. What does that say about *us*?

Monopoly Organized Force

That's what government is. Within the defined area it controls, government has a monopoly on power. And remember: Government has no assets of its own and creates no wealth. Everything it has is acquired by taking it by force from someone else.

Congressman Ron Paul has a little sign on his desk in his congressional office. It says, "Don't steal. The government hates competition." When I saw that I laughed. Because I knew it was true.

In asserting its monopoly on power, the government also places itself above the laws you and I have to obey. One hundred percent of the money the government takes in, it takes by force. That's theft. It lies to us constantly about where the money goes. That's fraud. And if it decides it's time for a "regime change" it starts a war and kills a lot of people. That's murder.

And one of the characteristics of monopoly organized force is the continual desire to increase its reach and power. It's instinctive. Just like your dog peeing on a tree or your cat clawing your furniture. It's instinct. That's just what they do. And by nature, government keeps feeding on its subjects until there's nothing left.

It has no particular desire to be good at anything, because as I demonstrated earlier in my analogy about spending a hundred dollars on a stranger, the government takes money from strangers and spends it on strangers -- other than what it keeps for itself.

The government can keep being bad at everything it does because it *does* have a monopoly. No competition. The government runs the railroads -- miserably. You can't start your own passenger train service because the government has a monopoly. After two hundred years, it still hasn't figured out how to deliver the mail without losing a small fortune every year. But you're not allowed to compete with it.

I know a lot of people aren't very fond of Microsoft, but if Microsoft had a legal monopoly on computers, they'd cost thousands of dollars and wouldn't be able to calculate two plus two. But competition in the computer industry is fierce, and because it is, the computing power of your hundred dollar cell phone is greater than that of main frame computers twenty years ago. Competition is good. It improves quality and lowers prices.

The government has no competition. It doesn't give a rat's ass how poor its services are or how much money it wastes. Because it's the only show in town and it forces you to do business with it.

And this brings us to the kinds of people who aspire to careers in "public service", which really means being serviced by the public. I'm not implying that everyone who works for the government is a bad person or has sinister motives. The bureaucracy is filled with people who have the misguided notion that they're actually doing something useful, and other people who just wouldn't be employable in the real world.

It's the ones who run for political office or aspire to powerful positions within the government. People generally gravitate to places where they can have a career that satisfies their personal desires. Musicians like to work in bands. Doctors work in hospitals. Animal lovers work for veterinarians. People who care about children go into teaching. People who care about culture and knowledge work in libraries. People who lust for power and control over others run for office or seek out powerful positions in government.

And to achieve the power they want, they'll tell you anything you want to hear. Most of them have a birth defect. They were born without a conscience.

In the market, the cream rises to the top. In politics, the scum rises to the top.

And there's probably nothing the government does that couldn't be done better and more economically in the free market. Think about it. Everything good you have, everything you like, you bought voluntarily in the market from people competing for your business. Everything that doesn't work, costs too much or is otherwise undesirable came from government. Probably ninety-five percent of what the government does could be done better and for less money in the market. And you'd have choices. Imagine that. But government's a monopoly. Government steals, and government lies. Because it can.

As I said before, it's instinctive for government to keep stealing and controlling until it finally devours its host. And that's about where we are today. There's not that much more to steal and it already controls almost every aspect of your life. Government is what the Mafia wanted to be when it grew up.

Government will never reform itself or voluntarily give up any power. But because it is, in reality, a fiction, willed into existence, *we* can will it right back out of existence. There are two ways to accomplish this: At the ballot box, which is easy. All we have to do is stop sending criminals back to engage in more mischief.

Don't reelect *anybody*.

Find honest people who really don't want to go to Washington and convince them to run. Demand that they conduct a repeal session of Congress. Make them start to undo the damage. And fast, before it's too late. Then two years later, vote *them* back out. A bloodless revolution.

The other way is messy. It would involve a lot of guns and become most unpleasant. I vote for the first method. It's only 546 people. What's so hard about that?

If we don't, very inconveniently soon, this country is going to bear a striking resemblance to the old Soviet Union. Or Nazi Germany. But worse, because now the government has really scary technology to keep us in our place. We're farther down that road than you think we are.

What About Our Children?

Don't we owe them more than we're giving them? Parents -- at least good parents -- want to raise their children to be good, happy and productive adults. And hopefully to have a better life than the one they were born into.

But we're saddling them with debt. Massive debt they didn't contract for and for which they will never see the benefits. They will forever be in debt for what the previous three generations did. How can they possibly find comfort and prosperity with the massive debt load we've placed on their shoulders?

Thomas Jefferson said the government should never incur debt that can't be paid off in one generation. He believed it was immoral to impose debt on people not yet born. And he was right.

If you took out a quarter million-dollar loan, spent the money on fancy vacations and high living, then passed away before it was paid back, would it be fair or moral to force your young children to be responsible for it? Of course not. Then why should they have to pay back government debt you allowed to be created?

And I believe parents need to step up and actually *be* parents. Anybody can be a father, but it takes someone special to be a dad. Or a mom. That's what our children need more than anything: A mom and a dad. Full time.

But it's more convenient to let daycare, preschool and the government schools raise our children and instill *their* values in them. It's not the government school's job to teach sex education. It's *your* job. Have you noticed that there were virtually no unwanted teen pregnancies until the government took over the role of teaching children about sex? Remember: The government gets what it wants. It's *your* job to teach your children *everything* important in life.

Are you even paying attention to what your children are being taught in school? Have you reviewed their text books? The average child receives a couple dozen shots and vaccines, in school. Do you know what kinds of medicine are being practiced on your children in school? Do you ask?

Our children are being desensitized and molded to become what the government and the big corporations would like them to be. As George Carlin said, quoted earlier, "...just smart enough to run the machines and do the paperwork, but too dumb to rebel."

In school, boys aren't even permitted to be boys. Or for that matter, girls to be girls. Natural and playful actions on the playground can end up with a fifth grader being taken away in handcuffs. Literally. It's happening.

And we don't even allow our children to be children at home. Our kids sit in their room with their head in a computer screen. Getting fat. Why aren't they outside playing? Exploring? Even getting into a little harmless mischief.

Everything's organized. Instead of putting together a little sandlot baseball team, where the fire hydrant is first base and the big maple tree is second, our kids get uniforms and driven to their organized recreation in the minivan, then driven back home. We don't even let them ride their bike without helmets and knee pads.

If you're younger than your intrepid purveyor of truth, let me tell you what things were like when I was growing up.

First, we were born to mothers who smoked and drank while they were pregnant. And they took aspirin, ate blue cheese dressing and didn't get tested for anything. We survived that.

We slept in cribs and played with toys covered with bright lead-based paints. And we survived.

Medicine bottles didn't have child-proof caps. We rode in cars with no booster seats, seat belts or air bags. And a big treat was riding in the back of a pickup truck. We survived.

We didn't drink water from a bottle; we drank it from the garden hose. And we shared sodas with our friends. We just passed the bottle around. We ate bacon and butter and drank Kool-Aid full of sugar. And we survived.

We played outside. All day. We built tree houses and go carts out of scraps. We climbed trees and fell out and got hurt. Getting hurt is how children learn lessons. We had sling shots, pocket knives, matches and BB guns. And we survived.

On weekends or during summer vacation, our mothers kicked us out of the house after breakfast and told us to be back in time for dinner. And we always found something to do. We were never bored.

We didn't have 200 channels on the TV cable. Nor did we have X-Boxes, video games, DVDs or cell phones. And we didn't have Facebook friends. We had *real* friends.

We were happy, and we weren't fat. So we didn't need Ritilin or Prozac.

This is how children grew up before the government and lawyers got involved *for your children's own good*. And before parents became obsessed with protecting them from everything normal in life. From all the things that teach them how to become grownups.

And as adults, our generation produced some of the best inventors, innovators, entrepreneurs, artists and musicians in history.

You need to find out what the schools are propagandizing your children with and make up for it by being good, full-time parents. And you need to let them go out side, all by themselves, and discover life on their own. If we don't our children are going to end up as fat, bored, depressed adults.

Deeply in debt.

In addition to that, they're going to have to be smart and clever enough to win their freedom back. Not a job for pampered, sheltered children with no practical life experience.

But How Will We Get Along?

The same way we did for this country's first 150 years. When we *were* free. When we *were* prosperous. When we *weren't* in debt up to our eyeballs.

The United States of America was the most free, most prosperous and most peace-loving country on earth until the government, the big banks and big corporations got their claws into every facet of our lives, stealing and hollowing out the soul of our existence.

Every program, agency and department I've critiqued in this book can be drastically cut back or totally eliminated with no harm to anybody other than the people who work for them. And those people can find something useful to do in the real world.

By ending the Fed, cutting taxes by trillions and balancing the budget, in very short order, this country can return to the ideals, ethics and morality that made it great.

It's all about freedom.

* * *

The problem is that just like the Soviet Union, eventually our bloated and inept bureaucracy is going to come crashing down on itself *and take us with it*. How big and bloated is it? The federal government writes *eighty million checks every month*. It must take a *really* big department to take care of that.

In Part Three, I'll be discussing what's coming, what you can do to stop it, and failing that, how to survive the aftermath.

Part Three is going to be pretty intense, so you might want to pour yourself a cold one before you turn the page.

"[W]hen you see that in order to produce, you need to obtain permission from men who produce nothing; when you see that money is flowing to those who do not deal in goods, but in favors; when you see that men get rich more easily by graft than by work, and your laws no longer protect you against them, but protect them against you...you may know that your society is doomed."

-- Ayn Rand, *Atlas Shrugged*

Part Three: Living in Amerika

Getting Started

The 2012 election will be the most important in this country's history. We have very little time to save what's left of our republic and begin to turn things around. And unlike elections past, this time your vote actually *can* count -- if you don't buy into the same lies you bought into in the past.

No Democrat is going to do anything other than finally drive the country over the cliff it's been racing toward for many years. And among the field of Republican candidates, so far, only *one* will put the brakes on before we hit the cliff. The problem is that we're so close to national bankruptcy and the certain resultant tyranny to follow, that even he might not be able to. But as of now, he is our *only* chance. I'm referring to Ron Paul, the congressman from Texas.

Disclaimer time: I have no association whatsoever with the Ron Paul presidential campaign. I met and *briefly* spoke to Dr. Paul on two occasions a couple of years ago and neither time did we even discuss politics. The following are solely *my* thoughts and opinions.

It's been said that politics is the art of compromise and I suppose it is. Politicians compromise all the time; it's the expedient thing to do. But a true statesman never compromises his principles. He holds firm for what he knows is right.

Compromise -- the selling out of principles -- is what got us where we are. Perhaps Ayn Rand said it best:

"When you compromise between food and poison, death will always win. When you compromise between good and evil, evil will always win."

Whether it's Ron Paul, another Republican not yet in the race at the time of this writing, or even a viable third party candidate, look for the one the media are demonizing, marginalizing or ridiculing. Vote for the candidate who will look you in the eye and tell you the truth. Even if it's not pretty.

Because an ugly truth is better than a pretty lie. That's your candidate.

2012 is beginning to look a lot like the presidential campaign of 1964 in which Barry Goldwater ran against Lyndon Johnson. In fact, it might be déjà vu all over again. Goldwater was the only non-establishment presidential candidate to win a major party nomination in my lifetime. He was uncompromising, not bought and paid for, and a strong constitutionalist.

He was considered a serious a threat to the powers that be, and throughout the campaign he was ridiculed, demonized and marginalized. The distortion and outright lies were something to behold. I can recall one story by the Associated Press, covering his appearances in Florida. "...only drawing spotty, unenthusiastic crowds..." I obtained a copy of the *St. Petersburg Times* the day after one of Goldwater's campaign stops there. In the *local* paper, on the front page, and in color, which was rare for a newspaper in those days, was a headline that shouted, "Goldwater draws the biggest crowd in the history of Al Lang Stadium."

So terrified of an honest man was the establishment, that one monthly news magazine even ran a cover story claiming more than eleven hundred psychiatrists had declared him insane. In the survey, which was highly unscientific even by the standards of the day, nearly half of the psychiatrists who responded judged Goldwater psychologically unfit to be president. They used terms like "megalomaniac," "paranoid" and "grossly psychotic," and some even offered specific diagnoses, including schizophrenia and narcissistic personality disorder."

After the election, Goldwater sued for libel and won. But of course the damage had been done. But the supreme Court's decision set a legal precedent that helped change medical ethics.

You may remember, or have seen the most famous TV political ad in history. It was the one showing a little girl sitting in the grass and picking petals from a daisy when a hydrogen bomb goes off behind her. The message, of course, if you vote for Goldwater, children are going to be blown to smithereens. Goldwater was called a war monger, but the peace candidate, Lyndon Johnson took us to Viet Nam and one of the longest and bloodiest wars in our history.

Just a little bit more of the history lesson, because it's relevant. What happened then is still happening today.

Senator Goldwater was also repeatedly accused of being a racist. Over and over again. That was a damaging accusation since the 1960s was the height of the civil rights movement.

But as is usually true, what you see on TV or read in the weekly news magazines is seldom the truth. The "racist" Barry Goldwater was responsible for desegregating the armed forces. His family business employed black people in numbers far beyond their percentage of the local population. He was also a lifetime member of the NAACP *and* an Honorary Indian chief. During his years in congress, he voted for every civil rights bill but one. The one he voted against was on constitutional grounds.

On the other hand, Lyndon Johnson, the media-proclaimed champion of civil rights, voted *against every* civil rights bill, even anti-poll tax and anti-lynching legislation.

Goldwater had very little financial support from the usual players. Almost all of his money came from individuals in the form of modest donations. He was even shunned by his own party. It was a true grass roots movement. Now, six decades later, it's time for another one.

The media lied then and they do now. Once the parties have nominated one of their anointed candidates the media will try to convince you there are great differences between the candidates. Predictably, CNN will favor the Democrat and Fox News will promote the republican. But it won't matter, because they'll both be bought and paid for.

Watch the news media's coverage of the candidates, and watch with a skeptical eye. Remember: Five multinational corporations control everything you see on television, and they're all inside players. Watch which candidates get the hostile questions and which ones get softballs tossed to them.

As always, most of the coverage will about the poll of the day. It'll be all polls all the time. And all the information you get from the candidates will be bumper sticker slogans. The candidates will be marketed to you like toothpaste.

And pay attention to fundraising. The news media tend to favor the candidates who raise the most money. Do some homework. Find out where the money comes from, because knowing where a candidate's funding comes from will tell what he's *really* going to do if elected. Mitt Romney, for example, has already raised tens of millions of dollars. From whom? Every one of those fat cat donors will expect something if he's elected.

Obama has bragged that he intends to raise a *billion* dollars for his reelection effort. If reelected, do you think he'll work for you or the people who gave him a billion dollars? The same will be true for any Republican who raises that kind of money.

Do an Internet search of the candidates' voting records in Congress or record as governor. Do the facts match the campaign rhetoric? Seldom. If they'll lie to get your vote, they'll lie once in office. Do they believe what they're saying or are they just holding their finger up to the political wind?

There's no time left for compromise. It's time to act. In the next election you'll have a chance to do something you possibly never did in the past: Vote for the person who *should* be president and not the one you think *can win*. If enough people vote for the person who *should* be president, this time the right person *can* win.

The problem with Republicans is that they keep voting for the person they think can beat the democrat. And every time, they've just ended up with *a democrat in Republican's clothing*.

Further, *don't reelect anybody*. Throw them *all* out.

Think of it this way: *Nobody* kept his campaign promises. *Nobody* honored and defended the Constitution. *Nobody* balanced the budget. *Nobody* lowered taxes. *Nobody* kept us out of trillion-dollar wars. *Nobody* stuck to his principles. So reelect *nobody*.

There's no one in congress who needs to be there, *including whoever you voted for last time*. And there's no one we could elect who would be any worse. And the less experience they have, the less mischief they'll get into.

Defeat them *all* in the primaries. **DON'T REELECT ANYBODY**.

While we out here were losing our jobs and our homes, and tightening our belts as we watched our savings and retirement funds evaporate, the average net worth among members of congress has greatly *increased* over the past year. Many members seeing their net worth double or triple *in one year*.

Besides the rampant corruption, members of congress are *allowed* to do insider trading. And since they're in on the game, they know in advance who the winners and losers will be. And they cash in. Still believe they care about you and your children?

"In matters of style, swim with the current;
In matters of principle, stand like a rock."

-- Thomas Jefferson

What Else?

Turn off your television. It rots your brain. I unplugged my television last year and couldn't be happier. If you do it, you might get a sitcom jones for the first week or two, but it'll wear off pretty quickly. Use your former television time for more productive things. Since turning off the TV, I've read an average of two books a week. And I've rediscovered radio and music. Or I just *do* things instead of sitting motionless for hours on end, staring into the electronic wasteland. You'll also save a thousand bucks a year in cable costs.

Get your news from the Internet while you still can. Behind the scenes in Washington, ruining the Internet is a high priority. When the Internet was developed, they had no idea what it would become: the world's free press. The Truth is on the Net and you know the government hates *that*. What the government wants is to turn the Net into a subscription service like cable or satellite TV, with *approved* sites.

Get off Facebook and Twitter. It's not socializing; it's just wasting time with trivial things. If you want to socialize, pick up the phone or go visit. And the CIA data mines Facebook 24/7. Every time you talk to a friend on Facebook, you're also talking to the CIA. And the NSA is tracking not just our telephone conversations, but our physical location, as well. NSA gathers an amount of information on all of us equivalent to the entire Library of Congress -- every six hours. For our safety, of course, because any one of us could be a terrorist.

Otherwise, prepare. Because unless we turn this around with the next election, our days are severely numbered. The country might survive a year or two, but possibly only a matter of months. That's how dire our financial condition is.

The total government and corporate debt in the country, including the unfunded liabilities, is more than *a hundred trillion dollars* and there's no way it can be paid. This country's *debt* is greater than *all the money in the world*. If we confiscated all the money on earth, it wouldn't be enough to pay the debt. Ponder that one for a minute. So a default is coming. There are two ways to default. We can either declare national bankruptcy and let our creditors (like China) come and gobble up everything of any value, or we can greatly inflate the money supply, which is another kind of default.

We just pay back our debts with worthless dollars. This hurts everybody. When something that cost you a dollar last year, costs a dollar and ten cents this year, your dollar lost ten percent of its value. A default of ten percent.

We keep hearing talk from the politicians and the corporate media about the economy turning around. But it's not and it won't. Because there's nothing to *cause* it to turn around. We don't magically go into a recession, then magically come out of it. Something *caused* it to happen and something has to *cause* it to end. And that something isn't and can't be the government or the Fed. The government has no assets other than what it steals from you, and the Fed has no money other than what it creates out of thin air.

Only the free market can bring a country out of a recession or depression. Business. Manufacturing. Trade. New jobs. But remember, we don't make anything any more. We need to end the Fed, balance the budget, bring the troops home, greatly reduce taxes and let the free market rebound and do its thing.

But because the odds, at this point, are better than even that this won't happen, you need to prepare for life as it's going to become. The economy in this country is far worse than the politicians want you to believe. Unless something is done, and soon, our economy is going to collapse. It could be a year or two. Or it could be a matter of months. When it does, it will be fast and without notice.

"*If the American people ever allow private banks to issue their currency, the banks, and the corporations that will grow up around them will, first by inflation, and then by deflation, deprive the people of all property, until their children will one day wake up homeless on the continents their fathers conquered.*"

-- Thomas Jefferson

When I write that our economy is on the verge of collapse, it's not my opinion. It's fact. Throughout recorded history gold and silver have been money. Or paper receipts for them. In other words, even paper money was based on gold and silver. And it was, at least in part, until Richard Nixon "closed the gold window" and devalued the dollar in one feel swoop back in the 1970s. That was the final nail in the dollar's coffin.

There are reasons why gold and silver have always been money. They can't be manufactured, they can't be destroyed, they can't be counterfeited and they're rare. Money has to *be* something. It has to have *value* that's universally accepted.

You can get yourself some nice paper and put a lot of fancy ink and official sounding words on it, but that doesn't make it money. It just makes it nice paper with fancy ink and official sounding words. A hundred dollar bill doesn't have any more intrinsic value than a one dollar bill. It just has two zeros added on. If nice paper with fancy ink were really money we could just print million dollar bills and pass them around. We'd *all* be rich.

Money has to be honest and has to have value that can be counted on. It has to be worth as much next year as it was last year. When paper isn't linked to something of recognized value, do you know what it's worth? Anything they say it is. It's just Monopoly Money.

I've always been amazed at how many people have told me gold and silver have no value of their own. They're just metal and metal isn't any more valuable than paper. But you know who knows the value of gold and silver? *Women.*

If you want to learn the difference between gold and paper, try this: On your wife's next birthday, go to your jeweler and tell him you want him to make a beautiful brooch -- out of paper. Ask him to make it the most beautiful brooch he's ever created and to wrap it in his best gift box. Take your wife out to dinner and while you're waiting for the dessert to arrive, take the gift box with the beautiful paper brooch out of your pocket, slide it across the table and say, "Happy birthday, dear. I had this made just for you to let you know how much I love you."

When she opens the box, the look on her face will teach you the difference between paper and gold.

I'll tell you who else knows the difference between gold and paper. All the central banks, including the Fed. The central banks are buying up gold as fast as they can get their hands on it. Gold for the banks, paper for us.

The United States, and much of the rest of the world have foolishly abandoned the gold standard and started printing paper money with no backing. It's called *fiat* money -- money by decree. And in an honest world, you might be able to get away with that, as long as the quantity of paper money was very carefully monitored and controlled. But we don't live in a very honest world.

But it's worse than that. We've gone past just printing paper money. The rise of the central banks (such as the Federal Reserve) has destroyed economies of many countries and ours is likely next. Because with a central bank such as the Fed, the entire economy becomes debt based. And the more debt that's created, the richer the owners of the Fed become. Because we have to pay the bank interest on every dollar it creates. The Fed creates a dollar from thin air, lends it to us, and receives interest on the "loan" of that dollar.

When it wants to heat up the economy it just prints and lends us more debt-dollars. In other words, it inflates the money supply, which is what causes prices to rise.

The news media, in true form, try to confuse us about inflation, with silly statistics about things like "inflation on the wholesale level". There's no such thing as wholesale inflation. When prices go up, it's referred to as the wage-price spiral, which is the *result* of inflation. Inflation is an increase in the money supply without a corresponding increase in goods or services. Too many dollars chasing too few goods. When that happens, prices rise.

Inflation is a big Ponzi scheme, and as with all good Ponzi schemes, the ones who start them make all the money. When the Fed prints a billion fresh new hundred dollar bills, everyone at the top gets to spend them first, while they're still worth something. By the time that new "money" works its way through the economy and trickles down to you, the prices have already gone up. Suddenly a tomato costs three dollars. Or ice cream doesn't cost any more, but what used to be a half gallon is now just a quart and a-half.

When the government gets out of control and can't stop spending money, or when people who can't afford houses want them anyway, the Fed is all too happy to lend the economy more "money". But eventually there's more debt than can ever be repaid. More government debt, more corporate debt and more consumer debt. But mostly government debt.

As I explained earlier, the government has no money of its own. Everything it has, it's taken from you. When we get to the point where it can't extract any more from you, it loses its only asset -- your income. Just like you or me, if the government gets to the point where it can no longer find a way to pay its debts, it has to go bankrupt.

Unlike those of us out here in the *real* world, governments have *two* ways of going bankrupt. They can go bankrupt like you or I can and just default. Or...they can start printing money, big time, which is often referred to as runaway inflation.

Our government is going to default. In six months, or a year. Sometime in the very near future. It has to; it's flat-ass broke.

I'm reminded of the story about a man in the park

sitting on a bench. An old friend he hadn't seen in a long time comes by and asks how he's doing. The man says, "Not too well. I went bankrupt." "Bankrupt?", says his old friend, "How did you do that?" The man replied, "A little bit at a time for a long time, then all at once."

And that's what's happened here. This country's been going bankrupt a little bit at a time for long time. Pretty soon it's going to be all at once. And when it happens, its going to be everybody out of the pool.

One way you can tell the government has no intention of stopping the runaway train is to watch how congress deals with what really *is* a crisis. As I write this, the news is filled with hysterical stories about the "debate" in the House of Representatives over raising the debt ceiling.

The matter of the deficit could be handled relatively easily, if the Democrats and Republicans had any intention whatsoever to actually address it. But of course they don't. The "debate" is just one more Washington puppet show. And if you still need proof that the Republicans are unabashed liars who only *pretend* to want smaller, fiscally responsible government, this is it.

The Republicans control the House. They could propose anything they want to. But the Republican and Democrat plans to deal with the debt crisis are nearly identical. Each one calls for trillions of dollars in new government spending and fictitious spending cuts in the future. The baseline budget calls for trillions of new spending with huge deficits as far as the eye can see, but each of the plans to deal with it involve cutting a only small fraction of the deficit -- sometime in the future. And they're not even cuts in spending; they're merely small reductions in the planned *increase*.

The "debate" has to be a puppet show put on for our entertainment, because it's absurd, even in the heart of Governmentland. Each party creating a plan nearly identical to the other, and each party ranting that if the other party's plan is adopted, unspeakable things will result. Actually, this could be one time they are telling the truth. Because no matter which plan passes, unspeakable things *will* result.

Let's say you were insolvent and facing the prospect of bankruptcy. Would your solution be to not only keep spending money as you had been, but to start spending more and to begin slowing down your spending sometime in the future? That kind of thinking would just ensure your personal bankruptcy. And that kind of thinking is going to ensure our national bankruptcy.

How easy would it be to avoid the coming bankruptcy? Do you believe the government spent *too little* money in 2005? Do you even *know* anybody who thinks the government wasn't spending enough money in 2005? The people who believe government spending was too low six years ago would form a pretty small club.

If we just rolled back spending to that level we could balance the budget *now* and would have no need to raise the debt limit. It would be that easy.

Ain't gonna happen.

So What's Going to Happen?

I have no way of knowing for sure whether we'll default in the good, old-fashioned way, or if we'll do it with hyper inflation. I'm betting on the inflation route. But either way, the economy is going to go into a serious tailspin. It's going to make the great depression of the 1930s look like a 'G' rated movie.

Assuming the government and the Fed choose inflation as the way out, and everything they've been up to in recent months indicates that's the road they've chosen, the economy is going to become chaotic. Prices will become highly unstable, many things will be in short supply or unavailable, jobs will be lost by the millions and all the savings of the middle class will be wiped out.

You can say goodbye to your 401K, your savings account, your pension, your mutual funds, your Social Security, your life insurance and anything else you thought was going to give you some future security. They'll still be there; they'll just be worthless. What good will be the fifty thousand dollars you have in your 401K be when a loaf of bread costs a thousand dollars? Suddenly your 401K will be worth fifty loaves of bread.

This will be the easiest way for the government to wipe out its debts. If it owes you a hundred dollars, it will hand you a nice piece of paper with fancy printing and official looking writing. The piece of paper will say $100 but in the marketplace it will be worthless. Debt paid but you got screwed.

That's how it's done. After decades of slimy, crooked and unconstitutional schemes and programs, the government will finally settle its debts by handing out worthless paper.

When it comes to this, crime will become out of control. No jobs, no welfare, not enough money for food. Even good people will go bad. There will be muggings and home invasions in numbers now unimaginable.

And there will be protests, some violent. And insurgencies. People organized, armed and determined to overthrow the government and restore the legitimate republic.

Oh yeah, it's gonna be a hot time in the old town tonight.

But there's going to be an even bigger danger: the government. The government's been planning for citizen unrest when the default comes. And it's been planning for a long time. You're not going to like what it has planned.

What the Government's Been Up To While You Were Sleeping

Throughout this book I've demonstrated that once the government (any government) goes beyond its moral and proper functions it becomes a criminal enterprise. Once it begins to rob Peter to pay Paul (theft), makes up ridiculous rules for you to obey (or be fined) or runs around the world spreading democracy (starting wars and overthrowing other governments), everything it does becomes mischief. Rather like teenage boys hanging out on the corner with nowhere to go.

The government has known for a long time where all of its spending and borrowing was eventually going to lead, and those with position and power have been positioning themselves to cash in while the rest of us suffer. The *powerful* politicians, the *big* banks and the *big* corporations are going to do just fine, for the most part. It's the way it always works. When the Soviet Union fell, suddenly there were billionaire oligarchs who owned everything of value.

The government always takes care of itself and its own. You're not in the club.

The government has been involved in all kinds of nefarious activities for many, many years. But when it tells us that 911 changed everything, it wasn't kidding. Since then it's been nefarious activities on steroids. Hundreds and hundreds of billions of dollars spent on things we're not even allowed to know about. When half of what government does is a state secret, you *know* it can't be good. The government justifies all its secret spending and secret programs by claiming "national security". Although to my knowledge, no one has ever defined national security. It's just one of those terms that sounds important. What national security amounts to is "don't ask and we won't tell".

Among the new government programs and hundreds of billions of dollars in spending to "keep us safe" are the following: Critical thinking time again. As you go through the list ask yourself if you really believe these things are designed to thwart terrorism, of if *just possibly*, there's a different agenda.

To keep us safe from the millions of members of al Qaeda hiding under every bed, the government now does the following:

Monitors *your* bank account activity, in real time. It's privy to every financial transaction you make. You no longer have any financial privacy.

Monitors every phone call you make, looking for certain "key words" that might indicate terrorist intent on your part. We're told the government will only pay close attention to people using those so-called key words. A while back I got to view the list of key words. Among them were "Elvis" and "truth". I'd hazard a guess that everyone in America says at least a couple dozen of the key words on a regular basis. So what it amounts to is that the government is claiming the right to listen to all of *your* phone calls any time it wants to.

The government also reads *your* emails and tracks *your* Web surfing activity. It can also track and monitor your physical location through your cell phone, thanks to mandated location tracking software built into your phone. For your protection, of course. It can further track you through the RFID chips embedded in nearly everything you buy and the GPS in your car. And if you think you're safe from that spy program because you don't have GPS, you're mistaken. Because every car sold in this country has GPS and has for a number of years. When you pay extra for GPS, what you're really getting is a screen on your dashboard so you can see it. The GPS was already there.

As you already too well know, if you want to fly you have to give up *all* your rights. And the nudie scanners and feel-ups are just the beginning. Presently the government is developing the next screening devices: full x-rays. In the not too distant future, you'll be getting x-rayed all the way to the bone. How much dangerous radiation to you think is floating around the airport terminals? How much will be? And the airport security is being expanded to include bus and train stations, as well.

There are now more than *thirty million* spy cameras in use in this country. The average American is on a spy camera twenty or thirty times a day. The cameras are at freeway entrances and exits and all over city streets. *Everything you do is seen.*

If you're a political activist and go to demonstrations or rallies, the government is there with you, taking *your* picture for its database of possible future trouble-makers.

Have you ever gone to Google Maps and looked at your house from space? Those are the images the government will allow you to see. It keeps the high-resolution images that can identify *you* from space, even read your license number.

And the government has developed spying devices so small that they look like insects. They can look, listen and be remotely controlled. If something that looks like a fly buzzes around *you* and won't go away, watch what you say.

The 2010 census demanded answers to questions that were nobody's business. But beyond that, if you were one of the holdouts, requiring a census taker to come to your house, he used his GPS device to upload the location of *your* front door. Because, presumably, anyone who resisted the census might be an enemy of the state and attempt to leave his house to go *somewhere* and do *something.*

As I wrote earlier, the CIA monitors Facebook all the time. It's also scanning your photographs with its facial recognition software and creating an electronic file on *you.* Presumably, sometime in the future, if you're in the wrong place at the wrong time, the government will find you.

If you decide to buy gold or silver, coin dealers are now required to keep *your* personal information on file. So if you've decided precious metals might be a good hedge against inflation or serve as emergency money, the government will know where to find it -- and maybe come and get it.

Electronic skin tattoos, already in use. Once this type of technology becomes widespread, the government will be able to monitor your location and activities of like never before.

In addition, this type of technology could one day become *mandated* by the government. For example, someday you may be required to have an "electronic skin tattoo" in order to prove your identity or to participate in commerce.

The FBI is now instructing store owners to report many new forms of "suspicious activity" to them. "Suspicious activity" now includes paying with cash. Hard to track you when you pay in cash instead of a credit or debit card.

Here's a nice one. "The Active Denial System". It works like an open-air microwave oven. When aimed at you it instantly heats your skin to 130 degrees, causing intense pain. The government refers to this as "the goodbye effect".

"Smart meters" are going into homes all over North America and Europe. These smart meters monitor your home every single minute of every single day and they transmit very sophisticated data about your personal behavior back to the utility company.

Our children are being trained to accept being under surveillance almost constantly. For example, the U.S. Department of Agriculture is spending huge amounts of money to install surveillance cameras in the cafeterias of U.S. public schools so that government control freaks can closely monitor what our children are eating. Since when is it the business of the federal government what your children are eating?

Now it's *pre*-crime. That's right, you might commit a crime *in the future*. The Florida State Department of Juvenile Justice has announced that it will begin using analysis software *to predict crime by young delinquents* and will place "potential offenders" in specific prevention and education programs.

And already, state police in Michigan are using "extraction devices" to download data from the cell phones of motorists that they pull over. This is taking place *even if those pulled over are not accused of doing anything wrong*.

LRAD sound cannons are already been used by law enforcement authorities to disperse large crowds inside the United States. They were used in Pittsburgh to disperse protestors at the G-20 summit. So how much "damage" can sound do? Well, it turns out that sound can actually do a whole lot of damage -- like permanent hearing loss. And because the sound cannons don't discriminate, innocent bystanders will also be injured.

The government now claims the right to enter *your* home while you're not there and rifle through your stuff. And it doesn't need a warrant or to tell you it did so. You no longer have any Fourth Amendment rights.

The government monitors *your* book purchases and library activities. If you read the wrong things *you* could be a terrorist, you know.

The government has federalized and militarized the police. Your local police now have a frightening level of firepower, which they're already beginning to use. Even against innocent people. These days, the police shoot first and ask questions later.

The government now makes up crimes as it goes along. Basically anything that inconveniences the government becomes an instant crime. One of these new crimes is taking pictures of any illegal or violent thing the government does. Catching it in the act is now a crime. It's now unlawful to take a picture of a policeman without his permission. So there you are on the street as a half dozen out of control cops are beating someone half to death. You now have to walk up to them and say,

"Excuse me. Do you mind if I take your picture while you do that?"

The government is developing exotic new weapons. Many of them energy weapons. Perhaps the spookiest of them all is a super-secret program called HAARP. The first HAARP installation was in Alaska. It now appears there are three or four more elsewhere. HAARP can blast incredible amounts of radiation into the ionosphere and presents a serious potential to do great harm to the planet. A lot about HAARP is not known since the program is so secret, but it's widely believed that HAARP is being used as a weather weapon. Google HAARP and see what you get.

FEMA camps. Why has FEMA established dozens of relocation camps around the country? These "relocation" facilities bear an eerie resemblance to high-tech prisons. In all, they're capable of housing millions of prisoners. Oops. I'm sorry. I meant refugees. Google FEMA camps and see what you get. Wild conspiracy theory? When I first heard about them I was skeptical. So I went to the official FEMA Website and found the page where it put the construction of the camps out for bid. The bid request was quite detailed: "...for the mass relocation of people and (those always spooky) other purposes."

Currently being quietly installed on our city streets is a new generation of streetlights. But these new streetlights do much more than light your way in the dark. They photograph you, eavesdrop on your conversations and can even talk to you. Zero privacy equals zero freedom.

And if the people get out of hand, demonstrating, rioting, whatever -- there are executive orders in place to declare marshal law. Marshal law is just a polite word for dictatorship. The executive orders have been printed in the Congressional Record and you can read them.

This country, and indeed, the world is headed toward a very dark and dangerous place. If these "Big Brother" technologies are not stopped now, someday these technologies will get into some very evil hands, turning day-to-day life into Hell on earth.

There's more. But this list should be enough to get you thinking. Yes, *critical thinking time again.* Go back through this list and ask yourself if you *really believe* these activities are designed to protect you from terrorists, of there just might be *another* reason. Does our own government consider *us* the enemy? Fear the government that fears its citizens.

Remember: Government *never* voluntarily gives up any power. And it doesn't matter how uncomfortable or unhappy you are, it's in power and intends to *stay* in power. And if you disagree or represent the slightest threat to its power, it has things it can do to you and places it can send you. How many innocent people did Hitler and Stalin round up? Between them, about *twenty million.*

You think it can't happen here? It can and does anywhere the people think it can't happen. You can hide your head in the sand and avoid reality, but you can't avoid the *consequences* of reality. When the economy finally splatters itself all over the pavement and the people react, the government will, too.

The billionaire oligarchs have been running this country, along with the puppet politicians, for years, and now they're about ready to cash in and reel us in if we object.

The real terrorists, from the *government's* standpoint, are the people who just want to be free and left alone.

So at this point, we have but three possibilities. We can effect a bloodless coup at the ballot box this time. We can hunker down and learn to live in the new reality, or we can avoid the coming reality and suffer the consequences.

My father once said to me, "There are three kinds of people in the world: a tiny group that makes everything happen, a slightly larger group who knows what's happening, and an enormous group that says, 'What happened?' He said, "You'll never be in the first group, but can always be in the second group." It was great advice and I've never forgotten it.

So your first line of defense is to really throw the bums out this time. Failing that, it's hunker down time.

What else can you do? Buy more copies of this book and give or sell them to everyone you know who might read it. Pass the information on. If everyone who reads this book gives or sells two more copies, before you know it, millions of people will have read it.

And it's not just this book. There has been a lot written, by many knowledgeable people on the same subjects. Each with its own take on things, but all leading pretty much to the same conclusion.

Learn. Then learn more.

And please get out of your mind that they're stupid and don't get it. Because they *do* get it. They're not serving *you*; they're serving *themselves*. It's all about sucking all the money out of the middle class and to the top. And by the looks of things they're doing a pretty good job.

What you can and should do depends on your current financial situation. Regardless, if you're in debt, get out as fast as you can or be sure you have enough liquidity (even in bad times) to keep up your payments. You'll want to own things no one can take away. I'm not counting your mortgage. Even if you default, the odds are you can keep living in your home for quite a while. But this is a great time to rent. You're never going to really *own* your house, anyway.

Learn to do things for yourself. The average American would probably starve to death if he lost his electricity for a couple of weeks. Because he doesn't know how to operate a manual can opener.

Buy *heirloom* vegetable seeds. You can find them on the Net. Store them in a safe place, or if you have space in your back yard, plant them. Learn to dehydrate and can.

Every week when you go grocery shopping, set aside ten extra dollars or so for food you won't be eating now. Buy and store non-perishable food that you *like* to eat. With some thought, you'll be amazed at the wide variety of food that has a long shelf life. If you have a freezer, you can also buy meat, fish, butter, berries, fruit juice and other things that will hold up for a long time if you vacuum seal them before freezing.

In all, you'll want *at least* six months worth of food stored.

Buy bottled water. I'd recommend the five gallon bottles because they cost less. Twenty to twenty-five gallons per person in your household should be sufficient.

Also stock up on personal care and paper products. They'll be in short supply and expensive.

Stock up on any prescription drugs you really need. And buy vitamins and create a first aid kit.

Buy four five-gallon gas cans, fill them and put them in a safe place.

Have emergency lighting and a good supply of batteries.

If you still have money after all this, lucky you. The next thing you'll want is a gun. Or two. Or three. *And plenty of ammunition.* For protection from a home invasion, the best gun to have is a shotgun, because you don't need to be a good aim. For personal protection, a pistol or revolver works best for obvious reasons. And a rifle for hunting. Depending on your lifestyle and where you live, think about what you might need for protection or the acquisition of food.

Buy two or three cheap prepaid cell phones. If you want phone privacy, use each one for a while then throw it away.

Next, gold and silver. Unless you have lots and lots of money, I'd recommend silver. You can buy gold and silver coins from any reputable coin dealer. You can ask for his advice, but I'd recommend one-ounce American silver Eagle coins. Don't tell people you own the coins and hide them well. And don't keep any more money in the bank than you need to pay current bills.

Still have some money left? Stock up on coffee, tobacco, sugar and vodka. More about this later.

And if you really want to prepare for the worst, buy a bugout bag. You can find them on Amazon or elsewhere on the Net. If things get bad enough you might really have to bug out for two or three days.

What if I'm wrong? I just gave you one of the *safest* investments you can make. If I'm wrong, eat the food, put the gas in your car, drink the water, use the toilet paper and spend the gold and silver. *The worst you can do is break even*, which makes it a pretty good investment in the current economy. In fact, you'll even make a little money. With prices going up ten to fifteen percent a year, and much faster in the near future, you'll be consuming them next year at today's prices.

Will things really get that bad? The Fed only has *one more rabbit left in its hat*. Inflation. Hyper inflation. That's the end game.

What does hyper inflation mean? Let me tell you a little story. I think we can all agree that the Germans are pretty smart people. So if it can happen there, it can happen here. And it *did* happen there in the 1920s.

The German central bank started inflating the currency to make it possible for the country service its debt. Before the inflation, Germany was a very prosperous country and a German mark was worth about the same as an American dollar. But the central bank was printing money so fast that its value rapidly declined. And I mean very rapidly. It got so bad that workers had to be paid twice a day because the money was actually worth less in the afternoon than it was in the morning. It got so bad that banks closed in the morning so they could stamp new denominations on the previous day's bills. It got so bad that at the peak of the inflation a loaf of bread could cost a million marks.

You may have seen pictures of Germans burning money in their fireplace because it was cheaper than buying firewood. The German inflation totally wiped out the investments and savings of the middle class. That's one of the crimes of central bank inflation. It's already happening here, but in Germany, it was happening and happening at lightening speed.

Suppose a German had purchased a one hundred thousand mark whole life policy, hoping to use the payout for his retirement? The insurance company was happy to write him a check for a hundred thousand marks -- and put a million mark stamp on the envelope. His entire life savings would have been stolen. Sadly, in this country, if we don't get things under control fast, the same thing will happen here. Because we have *trillions* of dollars in unfunded liabilities that can't be paid. Unless things change -- really change -- and soon, that's the only way they *can* be paid. And your hundred thousand *dollars* won't buy a loaf of bread, either.

How did it end? By the time it was over, if you had one American dollar, you could have bought Germany. *Germany wasn't worth a dollar.*

What happened next? Adolph Hitler happened next.

And history has a way of repeating. If A plus B has always equaled C, it will next time, too.

So...back to the good old USA. Why all this preparation? Because if -- no, make that *when* -- the economy finally tanks, things are going to get very different, very quickly. And not in very pleasant ways. Food could become scarce, very fast. It wouldn't take more than two or three days to empty the shelves in the super market. And there's an added danger. Once the bread basket to the world, this country has become a net *importer* of food. Yeah. We don't even make much of our own food anymore. When the dollar becomes essentially worthless, nobody's going to sell us any food, because they won't want to get paid in worthless dollars.

Having your own food reserves means you won't have to stand in line for government cheese.

Utilities could become undependable. There could be disruptions in the water supply. Or worse, sabotage. Same with gasoline. Are you old enough to remember the gas lines of the 1970s?

Everything I've recommended is designed to help you maintain a reasonably normal life in the midst of crisis. When the economy collapses, the new wealthy will be not being poor.

The guns. Personal protection. If you think crime is bad now, just wait. What's going to happen when a few million people already living on the edge lose their jobs? Or when the welfare checks stop coming?

And you never want to tell anyone you have these things. Even good people will do very bad things when they're desperate.

And you'll need to cultivate a new circle of friends. When things get so bad that everyone's figured it out, you won't know who to trust and who not to trust. Bad times change people. When times are really bad you'll want a circle of friends you can trust, who won't rob you or rat you out, who you can trade with and who you can rely on to help out in times of need.

These may or may not include your current friends. And on that subject, opening the eyes of any friends who are still in denial will prove beneficial to both of you. Seek out other people who know what's happening. You'll need them.

Why the gold and silver, and why the coffee, tobacco, sugar and vodka?

When no one trusts the dollar, gold and silver will be the money they'll want. It could very easily get to the point where *one* those silver coins you bought could pay your rent or make your car payment. Just one. And when people are desperate, they'll trade some pretty nice stuff for life's basics. One of those silver coins could be worth a pretty cool home theater, or all kinds of other things. There's the well-known story from the great depression of the 1930s, about the man who traded his Packard automobile for a couple hundred pounds of potatoes because he couldn't feed his family.

The other four things? Other than what you might want to consume yourself, they're great for bartering for smaller things. Coffee, tobacco, sugar and alcohol are all addictive. People will *pay* to get them when they're in short supply or unavailable.

How long could things be like this? Months. Maybe a

year. Maybe longer. *Will* they be like this? I wouldn't bet against it. Unless things *really* change, and soon, this is where we're headed. This is the inevitable result of all the things the government's been doing for the past several decades. But as I said before, if I'm wrong, you just eat, drink, drive and spend your investment. It's far safer than a mutual fund.

This is your first step in holding on to some of your freedom when most others will have lost all of theirs.

The Entire Book On One Page

Our founders fought a war with their oppressors and won their freedom. They gave us a federation of states and a constitution to protect our liberty, but as soon as we became free, people who weren't very nice (and there are plenty of those people in the world) started working to take our freedom and steal our wealth.

Slowly and insidiously the government increased its power and ability to tax. Along with that, the bankers finally managed to foist their central bank on us, allowing them to lend all money into existence at interest, and enabling them to become wealthy beyond imagination at our expense.

Greedy self-serving career politicians tell us anything we want to hear to get themselves elected to positions they abuse for their own interests. They pander to us, but serve their puppet masters. These politicians and the bureaucrats they empower have driven this country into the ground with trillions of dollars of aggressive wars and absurd government programs that benefit no one but those in control and their rich friends.

Now the handwriting is on the wall. We now have more debt than can possibly be repaid. Time is short and our only remaining option, short of bloody revolution, is to effect a *true* coup at the ballot box. We're not voting for president of the student council or head cheerleader; we're selecting the CEO of a very big country. Perhaps for the first time, we need to step up and vote like grownups.

Failing that, the only remaining option is to hunker down, protect yourself from what's coming and face the consequences of decades of giving the government a pass on all it's unlawful activities because we still had our BMWs and memberships at the racquet club.

It's now do or die time. What kind of world do you want to create for your children? Liberty and prosperity or tyranny and poverty? The choice is yours.

A Children's Story for Grownups

OLD VERSION:
The **ant** works hard in the withering heat all summer long, building his house and laying up supplies for the winter. The **grasshopper** thinks the **ant** is a fool and laughs and dances and plays the summer away. Come winter, the **ant** is warm and well fed. The **grasshopper** has no food or shelter, so he dies out in the cold.

MORAL OF THE OLD STORY: Be responsible for yourself.

MODERN VERSION:
The **ant** works hard in the withering heat and the rain all summer long, building his house and laying up supplies for the winter. The **grasshopper** thinks the **ant** is a fool and laughs and dances and plays the summer away. Come winter, the shivering **grasshopper** calls a press conference and demands to know why the **ant** should be allowed to be warm and well fed while he is cold and starving. **CBS, NBC , PBS, CNN,** and **ABC** show up to provide pictures of the shivering **grasshopper** next to a video of the **ant** in his comfortable home with a table filled with food. **America is stunned by the sharp contrast.** How can this be, that in a country of such wealth, this poor **grasshopper** is allowed to suffer so? **Kermit the Frog** appears on **Oprah** with the **grasshopper** and everybody cries when they sing, 'It's Not Easy Being Green.' **ACORN** stages a demonstration in front of the **ant's** house where the news stations film the group singing, **We shall overcome.** Then **Rev. Jeremiah Wright** has the group kneel down to pray for the **grasshopper's** sake. **President Obama** condemns the **ant** and blames **President Bush, President Reagan, Christopher Columbus, and the Pope** for the **grasshopper's** plight. **Nancy Pelosi & Harry Reid** exclaim in an interview with **Larry King** that the **ant** has gotten rich off the back of the **grasshopper,** and both call for an immediate tax hike on the ant to make him pay his fair share. Finally, the **EEOC** drafts the **Economic Equity & Anti-Grasshopper Act** retroactive to the

beginning of the summer. The **ant** is fined for failing to hire a proportionate number of **green bugs** and, having nothing left to pay his retroactive taxes, his home is confiscated by the Government **Green Czar** and given to the **grasshopper.** The story ends as we see the **grasshopper** and his free-loading friends finishing up the last bits of the **ant's** food while the government house he is in, which, as you recall, just happens to be the **ant's** old house, crumbles around them because the **grasshopper** doesn't maintain it. The **ant** has disappeared in the snow, never to be seen again. The **grasshopper** is found dead in a drug related incident, and the house, now abandoned, is taken over by a gang of spiders who terrorize and ramshackle the once prosperous and peaceful neighborhood. The entire **Nation** collapses bringing the rest of the free world with it.

MORAL OF THE STORY: Wake up or you could become the next ant. The inmates have taken over the asylum.

(Author Unknown)

Useful Resources

Books

Anything written by any of these authors will be well worth your time. Go to Amazon, key in the author's name and see what looks interesting. The list is in random order.

Robert Higgs
Walter Williams
Murray Rothbard
Ron Paul
Judge Napolitano
Thomas Szaz
Lew Rockwell
Ayn Rand
Gary North
Thomas Sowell
Frederic Bastiat
Karl Hess
Thomas Jefferson
Benjamin Franklin
George Carlin
Peter D. Schiff
G. Edward Griffin
Daniel Estulin
Mark Twain
Michael David Morrissey
Thomas E. Woods
Henery Hazlitt
David Ray Griffin
Bill Bonner
Jim Rogers
Gerald Celente
Doug Casey
Walter Block
Betty Akers
Paul Craig Roberts

There are many others but this list should provide a great start.

Magazines

Reason
Liberty
New American
Nexxus
Mother Earth News

Web sites

The following are Web sites I've found to be useful, informative and generally credible.

Alternative news

lewrockwell.com -- My favorite., thoughtful, intelligent writing.
infowars.com
rense.com
dollarcollapse.com
beforeitsnews.com
dailyreckoning.com
theintelhub.com
federaljack.com
activistpost.com
SHTFplan.com

All kinds of alternative news on a variety of subjects.

International news

rt.com

See this country and world affairs as others do, without the American filters. High quality journalism and very objective reporting.

Information on precious metals

kitco.com

All about gold and silver and current prices

Preparation Help

Americanpreppersnetworks.com
Survivalblog.com
Urbansurvival.com
Internet-grocer.net
Thereadystore.com
readymaderesources.com

Tips on getting ready for tough times

Natural Health

lef.org

The Web site for the Life Extension Foundation. A goldmine of information on orthodox and alternative medicine.

vitacost.com

Natural foods, vitamins, etc. at incredibly low prices. Wide selection and great service.

mercola.com

Dr. Mercola is a great resource for information on natural health.

Internet Privacy

Identitycloaker.com
Anonymouse.org
whattheinternetknowsaboutyou.com

Information on becoming invisible on the Net.

Personal Privacy

http://www.billroundsjd.com

Personal Protection and self Defense

www.danstarks.com

And while you're on the Net, Google the following and see what you get:

"FEMA Camps"
"Chemtrails"
"HAARP"
"Secret Government Bunkers"
"Facebook AND CIA"
"GMO Food"
"Federal Reserve Conspiracy"

And lastly, try this one: Google "Prescott Bush". The billionaire Bush family has been corrupt for along time.

Become your own investigative journalist. Use the net. If you find an interesting link, go there. And keep going. There's great journalism on the Internet. Is everything on the Net true? Of course not. But the truth is there if you keep looking. The truth isn't on the TV network news, no matter how long you look.

And for something different, buy, rent or download the following DVD: "America: Freedom to Fascism". Shortly before his death, Hollywood Film producer, Aaron Russo produced this eye-opening documentary about the IRS. The things you'll learn...

Between the time this book was written and the time it went to press, *more* very bad things have happened.

The Fed, which has been shrouded in secrecy since its inception, finally allowed itself to be *partially* audited for the first time ever. What was uncovered? During the "stimulus" the Fed created not two trillion, but *sixteen trillion dollars* ($16,000,000,000,000.00), which it spread all over the globe. Sixteen trillion soon to be worthless American dollars. We don't even know where it all went.

The government and the Fed want you to be stuck with Federal reserve notes, a wad of which one day soon will be worth less than a roll of toilet paper. In the meantime, the central banks are buying gold, because they know where their paper money is headed.

Meanwhile, back at the ranch, congress has been up to its usual shenanigans, passing a two trillion dollar-plus increase in the debt ceiling. The "negotiations" were just a big puppet show because the whole thing was a done deal from the beginning. Any time there's a bi-partisan deal, watch out. That's when both parties get together to do something *very* bad.

The media *spin* is that two trillion dollars is being "slashed" from the budget. But the *fact* is that the "slashing" doesn't begin until a couple more years down the road and the slashes aren't spending cuts, but a *slight decrease in the big planned increase*. Further, no future congress is even required to honor the deal.

The debt ceiling deal calls for *trillions* of dollars of additional deficits as far as the eyes can see, making a national bankruptcy even more of a certainty.

Nothing is being done to stop the coming train wreck and John Boehner is a total fraud. If his lips are moving, he's lying. and along with nearly everyone else in congress is a traitor to America.

The current world-wide debt crisis isn't the result of things out of control. Rather, it's being very well controlled. Trillions of dollars of soon to be worthless paper is circulating among the banking, corporate and government elite. They're buying up assets and stocking up on gold. When it's all over, all you'll have is their worthless paper. That's the plan.

And let's not forget the latest war to spread democracy: Libya. Another totally fraudulent and costly foreign military adventure. The war in Libya, fought by "rebels" who just happen to have millions of dollars worth of high-tech weapons, is just us and the banksters hiding behind the skirts of NATO.

The unprovoked attack on Libya isn't about toppling a ruthless "dictator". It's all about the theft of oil, gold and water, and forcing Libya into a debt-based currency like the dollar.

Want an eye-opener? Go here:

www.youtube.com/watch?v=Q11R56Y0Dx4

If it comes from Washington, DC and reported on the TV news, you can be pretty sure it's a lie.

2012 is your last chance to empty the whorehouse. If you don't Clean up the cesspool on the Potomac, get ready for your new life in third-world Amerika.

Rrrriiinnngggg! This is your alarm. It's time to wake up.